DARING NIAGARA

50 Death-Defying Stunts at the Falls

By Paul Gromosiak

Publishing Coordinator: Matthew Pitts

*The photographs in this book are from the collection of the
Local History Department, Niagara Falls (NY) Public Library.*

Address all inquires to:
Brian Meyer, Publisher
Western New York Wares Inc.
P.O. Box 733
Ellicott Station
Buffalo, NY 14205
(7 I 6) 832-6088

This book was published and printed in Buffalo, NY
ISBN: I-879201-23-2

Visit our Internet Site at
www.Buffalobooks.com

Contents

Publisher's Ponderings

Photo by Matthew Pitts

A ten-year-old boy tosses a small piece of wood the shape of a corncob over the rail into the mighty Niagara.

He struggles to watch as the twig bobs up and down in the current, his parents keeping a watchful eye on him as he clutches the railing and sticks his head into the cool mist. When he loses sight of the vessel, his imagination takes over. Or does it? Can he really see the branch falling — almost floating in slow motion — over the brink?

He pretends he's a Lilliputian passenger on the wooden vessel and imagines how it must feel to tame the frothy waters. Probably twice as thrilling as riding the Comet at Crystal Beach. Not that the boy would know; he's still too short to ride the roller coaster . . .

As a child, I never remember hearing about Anna Edson Taylor. Had I known about this widowed school teacher who became the first person to go over the falls in a barrel and live to tell about it, her tale would have ignited my imagination ever bit as much as that corncob-shaped boat that disappeared in the rapids one summer day in the late 1960s.

Taylor must have been one gutsy lady. I first read about her in 1984 as I was doing research for a local trivia game, my publishing company's first regional product.

Fourteen years and about 40 products later, the ghost of Anna Taylor floats back into picture as a key character in our latest book.

When Paul Gromosiak, my good friend and literary associate, suggested that his fifth book focus on the men and women who sought fame and fortune by tempting the raw power of the Niagara, I put the concept through my "interest filter," asking myself a simple question: would I be interested in reading the book?

You are holding the answer in your hands right now. For me, this literary safari has been a trip down memory lane. As a Buffalo journalist, I've found myself covering legal tug-of-wars and other daredevil developments.

There was Steven Trotter, a 22-year-old aspiring stuntman from Rhode Island who used a souped-up pickle barrel and packing used for nuclear warheads to test the fall's might.

There was John Paul Munday, a former skydiving instructor who, despite his fear of water, conquered the falls.

These are the stories that compromise Paul Gromosiak's fine work. I am honored to continue my role as Paul's publisher.

Creating a book is a team effort. Thanks to Matthew Pitts for his efforts as publishing coordinator and to Michele Ratzel, who has been our chief number-cruncher since 1991.

Our thanks also goes to John Hardiman and the entire staff at Petit Printing.

And finally, thanks to my parents for helping to instill in me an appreciation for the splendor of Niagara Falls and other local wonders.

For all of us who have perched at the edge of the Niagara, imagining what it might be like . . . read on.

Brian Meyer

Acknowledgments

T his book would not have been completed without the assistance of five special people: Maureen Fennie, Daniel Dumych, Eva Ehde and Helga Shultz — the staff of the Local History Department of the Earl W. Brydges Library, Niagara Falls, New York; James Neiss, professional photographer.

I also want to thank my dear friends for always being there for me. Thank you, Brian and Carol Sage; John and Therese Drozdowski.

Paul Gromosiak

To my brother,
John G. Gromosiak

Introduction

Why have men and women risked their lives performing stunts at Niagara Falls? Why tempt fate at such a wonderful place? Is it the ready audience? Is it the hypnotic lure created by the huge mass of falling water? Is there a simple answer to these questions?

No.

Some have done it for personal satisfaction. Some have done it to make an impression. Some have done it by accident. Most of Niagara's daredevils did what they did to become famous and make money. Fame escaped many, and money escaped most.

This book discusses fifty of the most interesting stunts. From barrel riding to bungee jumping, just about everything imaginable has been done at Niagara Falls.

After reading about the stunts, walk by the falls and gorge to see the places where they were done. Who knows? You might see another one being attempted. Undoubtedly, it is only a matter of time before another person adds his or her name to the roster of Niagara's challengers.

As of the spring of 1998, fifteen people have ridden in or on something over the Horseshoe (Canadian) Fall, ten of them successfully. Of the thirteen male challengers, two did it twice and five died. The two women survived.

As with other kinds of stunts, it is against the law in both Canada and the United States to go over the falls. Through the years, penalties for such risky performances have increased in severity because of the dangers to both performers and rescuers.

For want of a better term, those who have challenged the falls will be referred to as "waterfallers." Please bear with it. Thank you.

Man hath no glory here;
Watching in silence thy soul-waking wonder,
O Niagara! — hearing thy thunder,
Pride must not come near.

Jasper Barnett Cowdin
1886

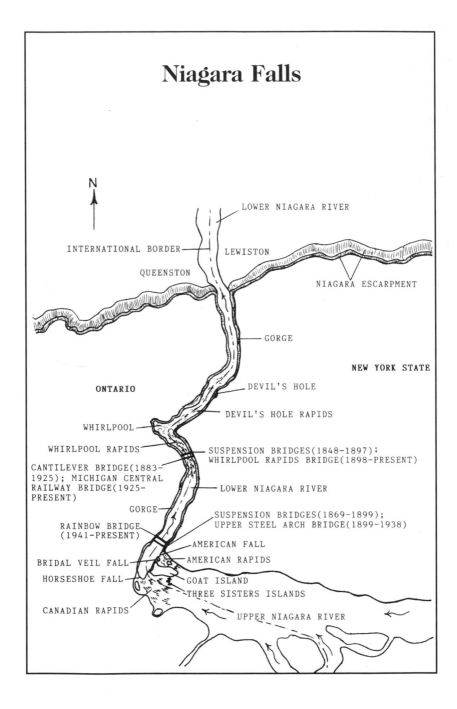

Niagara Falls

OVER THE FALLS IN A BARREL, BALL, BOAT

*"I will never go over the falls again.
I would sooner walk up to the mouth of a cannon,
knowing it was going to blow me to pieces,
than make another trip over the falls.*

— **Anna Edson Taylor**

The first person to go over the Horseshoe Fall in a barrel was a woman, Anna Edson Taylor. Most recently from Bay City, Michigan, this brave and mysterious widow hoped to become both famous and wealthy by doing what no one had ever done before. With the Pan American Exposition going on in nearby Buffalo, she was certain she would attract a huge crowd the day of her stunt.

Despite warnings from many people, including Canadian and American authorities, "Annie" was determined to ride in an oak barrel over the cataract sometime in October of 1901. She was able to get the assistance of local men, who, along with her manager, Frank Russell, inadvertently helped create a legend.

As it turned out, Ms Taylor ended up making her trip on her birthday, or so she said, October 24. Many people gathered to see her off that afternoon. Fully clothed, Annie was helped into the barrel which was then towed fairly close to the Canadian side of the Niagara river. With pillows over and around her, Annie was kept upright by an anvil at her feet. She was sure the one hour supply of air provided with an ordinary bicycle pump would be enough for the brief journey.

At 4:05 P.M., the barrel was released and bobbed its way into the spectacular Canadian Rapids. At 4:23, the unconventional craft plunged about 170 feet into the dense cloud of mist below the Horseshoe Fall. Onlookers struggled to get a good view of the lower river, wondering how much of the barrel and Annie had survived.

It took less than a minute for the barrel to appear. With little difficulty, it was pulled to shore. That was the easy part of Annie's rescue. Once it was determined that she was alive, efforts to pull her through the same hole she had earlier been stuffed through were quite

Annie Taylor selling mementoes of her trip over the Horshoe Fall

unsuccessful. The top of the barrel had to be removed. A saw was used to enlarge the exit.

When Annie was finally helped out, her only obvious injury was a bruise on her forehead, not caused by her perilous adventure, but inflicted by her rescuers' saw. Psychologically, she was somewhat incoherent, at first. This condition was probably brought on not only by the jarring in the rapids, but also by hypothermia caused by the cool water which nearly flooded the barrel.

Annie was not able to make a lot of money after her stunt. Her fame was short-lived. She ended up dying a poor woman.

"Nobody's got anything on me now."

— **Bobby Leach**

Bobby Leach was the first man to go over the Horseshoe Fall in a barrel. Like Annie Taylor, his age was never accurately determined. Unlike Ms Taylor, he was an experienced dare-devil and he made a fairly good living after the stunt. Leach had been a performer with the Barnum and Bailey Circus. On April 21, 1911, he jumped off the Upper Steel Arch Bridge. Just about two months later, on June 28, he rode in a steel barrel through the Whirlpool Rapids. He was really on a roll. Using a specially constructed new steel barrel, Bobby went over the Horseshoe Fall on July 25, 1911. He made it, but not without serious injuries. The following day, the Niagara Falls Gazette gave the following account of Leach's rescue.

"There was a rush to the barrel to ascertain whether Leach was living or dead. When the cap was taken from the barrel, the dull gray eyes of Bobby were peering out at the expectant group. There was a faint smile on his lips, livid from cold. On being taken out, Leach raised his arm toward the crowds lined along the river on either side and then almost collapsed in the arms of his friends."

It took Bobby about six months to recover from his injuries. Then he went on a tour of vaudeville theaters and lecture halls in the United States, Canada and England. Every place he went he displayed his barrel and showed a movie of his trip over the falls. The money just kept rolling in.

Leach returned to Niagara Falls, New York in 1920, where he operated a pool hall. In 1925, just before a vaudeville tour in New Zealand, he decided to prove he still had nerves of steel, even though he was an older man, probably in his sixties, by swimming across the lower Niagara River below the falls.

On August 30, wearing a red bathing suit, his first attempt had to be scrapped when a Maid of the Mist boat crossed his path, upsetting him. His second try was going well until his false teeth fell out when he gasped for breath. He tried to catch them, and in the process swallowed a lot of water and foundered. Apparently, that was enough for "Niagara's Hero." By the way, the man who accompanied Leach during this stunt and rescued him each time he failed was none other than "Red" Hill Sr., the Canadian riverman who had once been Leach's staunch rival at Niagara Falls.

In 1926, while walking down a street in Auckland, New Zealand, Bobby slipped on an orange peel and broke a leg. It became infected and gangrene set in. Poor Bobby died from shock during the operation to amputate the leg.

Bobby Leach and his barrel, with the Horseshoe Fall in the background

"If I thought there was a chance I would be killed
I wouldn't attempt to shoot Niagara Falls in a barrel.
But there isn't a chance.
I will be as safe in the 'Thundering Waters,'
as the Indians call the falls,
as I would be at home in Bristol.
I don't expect to be as seasick as I was coming
from England on the boat."

— **Charles Stephens**

People said Charles Stephens was invincible; that he would only die if someone shot him. Back in his native England, the Barber performed all kinds of stunts, even putting his head into the mouths of lions.

Dissatisfied with his profession, he decided he could make lots of money after going over Niagara Falls in a barrel. His confidence was buoyed by the successes of Anna Edson Taylor and Bobby Leach.

He had an oak barrel made in London. It stood 6 feet 2 inches high, and was encircled by steel hoops. For ballast, an anvil and lead weights were placed at the bottom. To protect himself, Stephens had the interior thickly padded. He had battery-powered lights and a three-hour supply of oxygen.

Despite the opposition of family and friends, Stephens and his barrel set sail for Canada on June 17, 1920. He arrived at Niagara Falls, Canada, July 6. Bobby Leach was on hand to greet him. After looking at the white and black barrel, Leach suggested it would not survive the trip. Stephens disagreed.

More negative comments did not deter Stephens. His journey began about 8:10 A.M. on Sunday, July 11. One of the barrel's hoops snapped off. The plunge took place at 8:55. Crowds soon gathered to witness the outcome of the unpublicized stunt. It wasn't until about noon that the result was obvious.

One by one, pieces of Stephens barrel were washed to the Canadian shore of the lower river. Then an arm wearing a distinctive tatoo was retrieved. The only other part of Stephen's body recovered was a rib.

"I can go over every day if there's any money in it.
Show me the dough, and I'll go.
I get more wise year after year."

— Joseph Albert "Jean" Lussier

On Wednesday, July 4, 1928, Joseph Albert "Jean" Lussier, 36, a French-Canadian who wanted to make a point and money, went over the Horseshoe Fall in a ball. Yes, a ball. Just before his stunt, he told people he was demonstrating that "some men, women and boys and girls with 'nerve' are needed" because of "the shape the world's in."

Lussier's ball was well constructed. It was built around two steel frames which had auto innertubes between them filled with oxygen. Covering the ball was a cord fabric and hard rubber. Six feet in diameter, the unusual craft weighed between 700 and 1,000 pounds with Lussier in it.

Even though the stunt was advertised, it was still not permitted by the authorities, so Lussier and his assistants had to be elusive in order to enter the upper Niagara River. A huge crowd of about 200,000 gathered along the shores.

Lussier started his trip about five miles above the falls. His ball bounced through the Canadian Rapids and went over the brink of the fall easily. About a minute later, it appeared in the lower river and began to float downstream. It was caught by rescuers in boats and brought to the shore.

Jean had a scratch on his face when he came out of the ball. Otherwise, he was quite well, physically and mentally. Indeed, he was a man of "nerve."

After touring with his ball and movies of his trip, Jean settled in Niagara Falls, New York, where he spent a number of years during the summer months displaying his ball in the Niagara Falls Museum and working in the tourist trade. He sold pieces of the inner tubes from his ball for 50¢. Some say he used other inner tubes long after he ran out of the originals.

In the 1940's, Jean decided to help his country by working in an industrial plant. There he worked until he retired at 65. He died in his 70's probably feeling quite proud of himself.

"If I die,
the turtle will carry the secret of the trip
and reveal it at the proper time."

— **George L. Stathakis**

George Stathakis was probably the strangest person to make a trip over the falls in a barrel. He was a writer and "philosopher." Much of his writing didn't make any sense and his idea of philosophy included "conversations" with Plato and Socrates. He had a pet turtle, "Sonny Boy," who was over one hundred years of age and, according to Stathakis, could talk.

At 46, George was old enough to know better, but he felt a trip over the falls would add immeasurably to his wisdom and thinking. In February of 1930, he announced to the press his intention to make the trip in a rubber ball. He ended up constructing the largest wooden barrel ever used to go over the falls. It was made of oak staves, four inches thick, held in place by strong steel hoops. The ten-foot long barrel had steel "bumpers" at each end. Stathkis had padding and an air mattress inside, along with straps and a steel casing. A three-hour supply of oxygen was thought to be enough for the journey.

On Saturday, July 5, 1930, at about 3:25 P.M., Stathakis' red, white and blue barrel began its illfated ride through the Canadian side of the upper Niagara River. Stathakis and his pet turtle had a rough ride through the Canadian Rapids. At about 3:35, after pausing for a second or two at the brink, crowds cooed as the barrel plummeted into the misty abyss. It didn't come up.

As the day ended, the crowds dispersed and George's rescuers waited until about 4 A.M. of the following day. It wasn't until 1:30 P.M. on Sunday that the barrel was recovered from the lower river. It was damaged but intact. Inside, the turtle was alive, but George was dead, asphyxiated by a lack of oxygen.

Sonny Boy lived for a long time at the Niagara falls Museum. It was quite a curiosity, but it never said a darn thing to anyone. It probably only talked to its late master.

"I don't think there is much risk,
I figure the trip will take about ten minutes,
and while it will be rough, I'll make it okay."

— William "Red" Hill Jr.

I n July of 1950, William "Red" Hill Jr. announced to the press that in 1951 he would go over the Horseshoe Fall in a ball similar to the one used in 1928 by Jean Lussier. That same month, his younger brother, Lloyd, failed in his attempt to go over the falls in a steel barrel. Only suffering from frustration, Lloyd was caught in a weir used by a Canadian power plant. After he was taken out by rescuers, the barrel was released and went unoccupied over the falls.

The Hill brothers were sons of William "Red" Sr., who was a man who knew the Niagara river very well. Unlike his sons, he never attempted a trip over the falls, but he did other daring things in the river, including the rescue of many living and dead people. "Red" Jr. and Lloyd claimed they also knew the river well. Let the historical record judge them.

"Red" Jr. followed through with his prediction, but he changed his mode of transportation from something secure to something extraordinary. For want of a better name, he called his invention the "Thing." Some people referred to it as a "rubber ball," which it really wasn't. It was made basically of 13 rubber truck tire non-blowout inner tubes lashed together with a heavy canvas and a thick net. The ends of the "Thing" were packed with smaller air-filled inner tubes. To keep Hill from being bounced around, he was surrounded by still more air-filled tubes, one of which was equipped with a hose and mask so he could get some air if needed.

Did the authorities try to stop him? No. Despite ordinances against such foolishness, Hill was allowed to advertise his stunt. This attracted a huge crowd of about 200,000.

Hill didn't do it for fame or personal satisfaction. He, like so many others, did it for fortune.

Despite his expressions of confidence in himself and his "Thing," Hill brought some charms and good luck pieces with him. The 38-year-old man had a four leaf clover, silver dollar, small doll, a bit of the famous blarney stone and many other things. What he didn't have with him was enough good sense.

At about 2:30 P.M., on Sunday, August 5, 1951, Hill rode in the boat towing his "Thing" out to a point about five-eighths of a mile above the Horseshoe Fall. At about 2:50, the "Thing" with Hill inside it began its trip through the beautiful and dangerous Canadian Rapids. At about 3:03, the dancing and whirling "ball" made its historical plunge.

The onlookers gasped in horror as the much mutilated "Thing" appeared below the cataract. It had literally fallen apart. Red's shoes were still tucked in one end of the "ball," but Red was no where to be seen. His battered body was recovered from the Maid of the Mist pool (the part of the lower Niagara river on the Canadian side, just before the Maid of the Mist dock).

Red's brother, Lloyd, told the press that he would make another attempt to go over the falls "next week, in the first barrel I can get my hands on." He never did it. Apparently one tragic death in the family was enough.

The challenges to the Niagara River and its falls by members of the Hill family should in no way overshadow their many contributions to the welfare of other people, both residents and visitors, many of whom owed their lives to them. The Hills had also for many years assisted the authorities in retrieving bodies from the river.

"An IBM employee would not engage in this sort of thing from what I understand, they wear white shirts."

— **William Fitzgerald, alias Nathan Boya**

William Fitzgerald, alias Nathan Boya, was the only African-American to go over Niagara Falls in a barrel. Actually, his craft was a large rubber and steel ball, about 10 feet in diameter. It was similar to Jean Lussier's, but much more secure. In case he might end up below water for a long time, Boya brought along with him 13 cannisters of oxygen.

The 30-year-old man was from the New York City area. It was rumored that he worked for IBM, but that and other facts about him were never certain. He said he went over the falls because he just had to do it. Some members of the press thought he did it for romantic reasons, to supposedly impress a woman from his past. One thing is for sure, he didn't do it for fame and fortune.

After sneaking his "Plunge-O-Sphere" from New York City to Niagara Falls, he managed to elude authorities and enter the river on the morning of July 15, 1961. While bouncing and bounding his way

Nathan Boya's rescuers getting ready to take him out of his ball

through the Canadian Rapids, he opened the hinged door on the top of the sphere, to check his progress he later said. He described his adventure very well. In his own words:

> "As my ball began speeding down the current toward the deadly Horseshoe, the Sphere held me calm and confident within. Suddenly my vehicle was falling through the air over the first 50 foot drop in the turbulent upper rapids. Just as suddenly, my more than half ton of rubber and steel crashed against a rock. I felt the awful shudder of the frame as my body strained against the safety belts, while the ball gave, bounded back, and thumped on into the rapids, partly split by the blow. Fear spiraled in me, seeding my mind with doubt and terror. The rumbling crest of the great Falls was still ahead, hidden under an overriding heave of continuous thunder. Finally, I clawed overhead for a grip with which I could try to hold the top closed by hand — just as the Sphere was swept over the brink. Down we went, the Sphere and I, deep into the violence of the lower basin."

Boya received only a few minor cuts and bruises. Before his sphere was taken back to the shore below the falls, he opened the door and waved to the people standing at Table Rock, the viewing point by the Horseshoe Fall on the Canadian side of the falls.

Another distinction Boya is noted for at Niagara is not at all positive. He was the first person to be fined by the Canadian authorities for stunting — a meager $113.

Fitzgerald has returned to Niagara Falls more than once since his stunt. While visiting in 1988, he told the press that he was going to be the first person to go over the falls twice. This time he gave a definite reason, to protest the treatment of women and minority scientists. He never did it.

"I'm now the last of the Niagara Daredevils,
and if someone else should come and do this tomorrow,
I'd probably come back the next day
to make another trip over."

— Karel Soucek

On Saturday, June 11, 1977, at about 4:00 A.M., Karel Soucek, a 30-year-old Canadian, rode inside a discarded oil tank from below the Rainbow Bridge to the Whirlpool. He made it unharmed, but he was taken to Niagara Parks police headquarters and charged with performing an act without a permit and illegal launching of a water craft.

The barrel Soucek rode through the lower river and Whirlpool Rapids was much more than a simple oil tank. Inside it were a bucket seat, electric lights and a citizens band radio.

In the summer of 1983, Soucek told the press that he planned to go over the Horseshoe Fall in a custom-made metal and plastic barrel. It wasn't until the following year that he actually did it.

On Monday, July 2, 1984, he went over the falls with little fanfare. Documenting the feat were professional photographers, who

Karel Soucek's barrel about to go over the falls; note his notes and signature

filmed the entire journey. Soucek hired them because he intended to make a bundle of money from his stunt.

Because of its sophisticated construction, including many safety features, Soucek's barrel was just about guaranteed a successful trip. Soucek survived with only a few minor bruises. He thoroughly enjoyed the limelight for awhile. His confidence was at an all-time high.

By November of 1984, Soucek was making a lot of money from his ride. He hoped to make at least a million dollars by the one-year anniversary of his stunt. He made a comment that was eerily prophetic, saying, "so far, I'm young enough to make it a success, unless I slip on a banana peel."

On Sunday, January 20, 1985, a Thrill Show and Destruction Derby was going on at the Houston, Texas, Astrodome. Soucek was set up to recreate his plunge over Niagara Falls. He was inside a specially designed barrel placed about 180 feet above a tank of water about 9 feet deep and 12 feet wide.

When Soucek's barrel was released, it spun out of control and missed its mark, striking the rim instead of the center of the tank. Poor Karel lived for awhile, but his injuries were extremely critical. He died in a local hospital. The "Last of Niagara's Daredevils" had performed his last stunt.

"It was like an elevator with no cable."

— **Steven Trotter**

The youngest person to ride in a barrel over Niagara Falls was 22-year-old Rhode Island native Steven Trotter. His first attempt to do the stunt was in November of 1984. He was stopped by the authorities just as he tried to put his barrel into the water above the falls.

Trotter spent thousands of dollars to construct his fancy craft. It was made of modified plastic pickle barrels lined with the same kind of foam used to ship nuclear warheads. It was reinforced with a dozen layers of fiberglass. Surrounding the barrel were 6 inner tubes from tires used by earthmovers. Trotter could communicate with his assistants using a walkie-talkie. He also hired a film crew to videotape his trip.

On Sunday morning, August 18, 1985, Trotter was eager to get the stunt over with, hoping to start about 6:30. He was wisely convinced to wait until after 8:00 A.M., because at that time more water would be released by the power authority into the rapids above the falls. Had he gone over before that time, he stood a good chance of being killed because of more rocks above the water both above and below the falls.

Trotter's adventure was quite successful. He only suffer minor bruises. His blue craft had the NBC peacock on it for a very good reason. He was hoping to be booked on the Johnny Carson show. He also hoped to make money selling teeshirts and copies of the video-tape. What he really wanted, however, was to become a real stuntman. To do that he needed to attend a proper school.

Trotter did appear on the Johnny Carson show on Friday, August 23, 1985. Describing his tumble over Niagara Falls, he said, "I went over at about 70 miles per hour and I think it was the nuclear warhead packing that saved me. I had two 160 pound sandbags in the end of the barrel and I figured I'd go over feet first, but instead I went over head first. I was in the river and it was all quiet, then . . . wham!"

Trotter didn't make a lot of money selling mementoes. In fact, he ended up paying the largest fine, up to that time, ever paid by a Niagara daredevils — a whopping $5,000.

As Johnny Carson might have said, "stay tuned, we'll be right back." Trotter would not return to Johnny's show, but did return to Niagara Falls. More about that later.

"I've done a lot of things in my lifetime
that I think are equal to Niagara Falls.
Anyone who can jump out of a plane at 17,000 feet
can do the falls."

John David Munday

On Sunday, July 28, 1985, John David Munday, a man who admitted being afraid of water, tried to go over the Horseshoe Fall in 400-gallon plastic tank covered with 10 inches of styrofoam. At each end of the barrel was bulletproof glass.

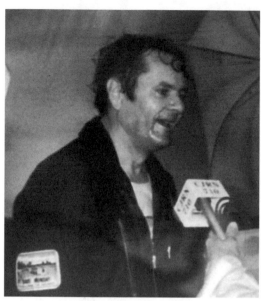

John David Munday just after his trip over the fall

The former sky-diving instructor entered the water in a bad spot, for two reasons. First of all, had the authorities not thwarted his stunt, the current there would naturally have taken him back to the shore. Second, the colorful barrel was easily spotted in the water by the police, who notified Ontario Hydro, and it only took them a few minutes, using the water control dam in the upper river, to lower the water where Munday's barrel floated.

Grounded and frustrated, Munday and his barrel were removed from the river. On the barrel was the inscription, "To Challenge Niagara, July 1985." Planning another attempt, all Munday had to do was change the date.

On Wednesday, August 28, 1985, he was fined $503 in Ontario Provincial Court for attempting to perform a stunt at the falls. He was also placed on a two-year probation and warned that another try at the falls could coat him $1,000 and land him in jail for up to 30 days.

Guess what? On Saturday, October 5, 1985, he returned to the scene of his "crime." Using the same barrel, he made it this time. Describing the plunge, he said, "I was knocked out for two or three minutes. I can remember just asking, 'are we over yet?'" (He had a two-way radio with him.) Both he and his barrel survived with only minor damage.

Munday paid a fine of $1,500. He was also warned about any more stunting.

In 1987, after a successful ride through the Whirlpool Rapids in a barrel, he stunned everyone by announcing that someday he planned to challenge the American Fall, rocks and all.

*"We wanted to show these kids
there's a lot better things for kids to do
than be on the brink of dope.
Go on the brink of the falls.
You'll see what a high is all about."*

Jeffrey Petkovich

In 1988, two Canadians, Peter DeBernardi and William Hill, announced to the world that they were going to be the first duet to go over the Horseshoe Fall in a barrel. They said it was a part of their campaign against drug abuse. Hill later had a change of heart after having bad dreams about the stunt.

DeBernardi was determined to find another partner, and he did, another Canadian, Daniel Ray. That was in April of 1989. After a lot of publicity about the stunt, Ray pulled out.

DeBernardi then tried to talk experienced Niagara waterfallers, namely Dave Munday and William Fitzgerald, into accompanying him. Both refused.

Finally, 42-year-old DeBernardi found a partner, 24-year-old Jeffrey Petkovich, another Canadian. They planned to go over the falls in September of 1989.

The barrel was a 12-foot reinforced steel tank. Weighing about 3,000 pounds, it contained two oxygen tanks, hammocks with straps, Plexiglas windows and a video camera to film the stunt. On the side of the barrel was a slogan, "Don't Put Yourself on the Edge — Drugs Will Kill." The men lay inside, head-to-head. Only one could sit up and look out of the window.

On Wednesday, September 28, at about 4:30 P.M., DeBernardi and Petkovich entered their craft. Then their crew launched it over the cement and steel railing nearly 200 yards from the brink of the Horseshoe Fall. Tourists watched the spectacle in bewilderment. Canadian authorities were not there to stop the stunt.

At about 5:30, the barrel went over the flank of the falls, striking some rocks. Fortunately, no serious damage was done to the craft or crew.

Describing the brief journey, DeBernardi said, "when she was launched into the water, I felt no sensation. It was like floating in a boat. Going over, there was no sensation at all. We didn't even know we hit bottom. It was just a free fall."

Petkovich's description was a bit different, saying, "it felt like a roller coaster ride, falling straight down. But with a roller coaster ride, you come to a minor stop, you feel it — but not as much as we did."

When Petkovich came out of the barrel, all he was wearing was a pair of cowboy boots, a green necktie and a white cowboy hat. That's all he had on. In one hand he held a pack of cigarettes. The other hand held a can of beer which he proceeded to shake and then spray the contents on his rescuers.

DeBernardi and Petkovich ended up paying Canadian authorities a fine of $2,000. Petkovich said he never wanted to go over the falls again. DeBernardi said he'd like to do it again — perhaps even go over the more dangerous American Fall.

"He lived to kayak."

— Friends of Jesse Sharp

At about 1:30 P.M., on Tuesday, June 5, 1990, a kayak was spotted in the Canadian Rapids, and someone was in it. The person paddling the small craft was 28-year-old Jesse Sharp, from Tennessee. He appeared to most observers to be determined to go over the falls.

As soon as Canadian park police found out about the kayak, they told the people in the control room of the water control dam above the rapids. Using 18 gates, it was possible to nearly turn off the water going over the Horseshoe Fall. Sharp was very good at controlling his boat, avoiding the ever increasing shallow places and rocks. Was it a stunt? Was it a suicide?

Jesse Sharp was an experienced kayaker, mastering dangerous rapids and smaller falls in other places. He and his friends thought he could survive the plunge over the cataract *and* the trip through the rapids in the gorge, all the way to Lewiston. So confident was Jesse that he left his car parked at Artpark with the keys in it. He even had plans for dinner the day of the stunt.

Just as Jesse approached the brink of the Horseshoe Fall, he confidently raised his arms and oars over his head. Was he celebrating victory? Was he waving to the onlookers? Was he resigning himself to his fate? We'll never know.

A little later the same afternoon, the kayak, which had the word "Rapidman" on it, was found below the falls, undamaged except for a dent near its cockpit. There was no sign of Jesse. His body was never found.

Later, some experienced kayakers complained that, had the water not been lowered in the Canadian Rapids, Jesse might have been able to clear himself from the more dangerous waters in the plunge pool just below the falls. Perhaps. Perhaps not. According to Karen Seifert, and interpretive naturalist for the New York State parks, "the more water, the faster it goes. But I think Ontario Hydro did exactly right. If he (Sharp) was counting on that forward speed (to carry him away from the falls), he would have lost it. I don't believe that he would have survived anyway."

"Anyone who would go over the falls twice would have to be crazy."

— **John David Munday**

On Sunday, July 15, 1990, at 4:30 A.M., John David Munday began his attempt to be the first person to go over Niagara Falls in a barrel two times. He and his crew hurried to get the barrel into the rapids above the Horseshoe Fall. What everyone failed to consider was that the water going over the falls at that time in the summer was very low, about 25% of the normal flow. Water was being diverted upstream and sent to the reservoirs above the Canadian and American power stations.

No sooner was the barrel in the rapids, it stopped in a shallow place. Somehow, Munday was able to roll it over. It moved again but came to a halt about one foot from the brink of the Canadian flank of the waterfall. So there he lay in his craft, frustrated and perilously close to a certain drop onto the rocks and boulders below.

Working in a constant rain, Munday's rescuers risked their lives to save his. His barrel was hoisted out of the rapids. By 7:00 A.M., he was taken out of it.

In December of 1990, Munday was fined $4,000 for his failed stunt. His reaction was, "I got off lucky. That's a super deal. I was expecting $10,000."

Munday wasn't deterred by the fine. "The next time I go I'll get over, though," he said.

At 8:35 A.M., on Sunday, September 26, 1993, riding inside a converted diving bell emblazoned outside with red maple leaves, Munday made his second trip over the Horseshoe. His reaction was jubilant. "Three years I've been waiting for this. Three years," he said.

He didn't make the second trip just to be the first. In November of 1993, he told the press that he did it to thumb his nose at the media. Quoting him, "because in '85 you guys (the press) all said I used a high-tech barrel, (that) I didn't have the nerve to do it in an old-fashioned thing. I cursed the media when I went in the river this time. You tell me if it was high-tech." In a report about his stunt the day after it was done, a local paper did refer to his barrel as "low-tech."

"I just like to have fun, you know.
I think positive thoughts only — no negativity in my life."

— Steven Trotter

Guess who else returned to Niagara Falls? On June 18, 1995, Father's Day, Steven T. Trotter, now 32, decided he had to go over the Horseshoe Fall again, but not alone. With him this time was a friend, Lori Martin, 29. An entourage of family and friends served as assistants.

The barrel was basically two water heaters welded together, then wrapped in Kevlar and expansion foam. Weighing about 1,100 pounds, the $25,000 craft contained two air tanks. Trotter and Martin lay feet-to-feet, and each wore shoulder harnesses and bicycle helmets.

The daredevils began their trip about 8:45 A.M. By 9:00 they were over the falls. Unfortunately, the barrel became lodged in rocks just below the falls. While their air supply was running dangerously low, rescuers risked their lives to secure the barrel and get Trotter and Martin out. Neither had any serious injuries.

They were the first of Niagara's challengers to spend time in jail. Canadian authorities were much harder on them than their predecessors. Martin paid a $2,000 fine, while Trotter paid $5,000.

On November 12, 1995, Trotter fell from a tree in Florida, breaking his back. He must have healed well enough to take more chances with his life. On April 27, 1997, he and three others were injured bunjee jumping from a bridge in Florida. Some people never learn.

"I'm gonna go out there
and give it my best shot
and see if I can make a difference
in the United States,
especially (for) veterans."

— Robert "Firecracker" Overacker

At about 12:30 P.M., on Sunday, October 1, 1995, Robert "Firecracker" Overacker, 39, a stuntman from California, tried to draw attention to the plight of the homeless in the United States by riding a Jet Ski over the brink of the Horseshoe Fall.

Overacker was a very confident man. Despite warnings from people who knew about the character of the falls, he truly believed he could survive the unique performance.

Prior to his stunt, Overacker told the media, "I think the homeless situation in this country has to be rectified. In less than an hour, I am going to drive my Jet Ski off the end of Niagara Falls." He thought his deed would make people say, "Gee, if that guy was willing to risk his life . . ."

At the brink of the falls, Overacker was seen in the air above his falling craft. He raised his left arm. He intended to get down safely by using a rocket-propelled parachute. The rocket fired, but the chute didn't open. Overacker fell 170 feet to his death. His body was later taken from the lower river. The Jet Ski floated upside down in the river for awhile; then it sank.

Across The Gorge On A Rope Or Wire

Funambulists are tightrope walkers. Much of the second half of the nineteenth century was their heyday at Niagara Falls. During that era, nearly every summer there were ropes or wires stretched out across the scenic gorge below the falls.

Just about everything imaginable was done to entertain the demanding crowds. As dangerous as the stunts often were, only one person died from a fall, and that happened when he went on his rope without an audience.

The first funambulists set up their ropes relatively close to the falls, where the gorge is quite wide. The rest of them set up further downstream, where the gorge is more narrow. The updrafts by the falls had also been a problem.

In recent years, some funambulists have wanted to perform over the gorge, sometimes with the blessings of local politicians and businesspeople. The commissioners of the American and Canadian parks have not yet given their blessings.

*"There be one American falls,
and one Canada falls;
when Blondin falls
there will be one French falls."*

— **Jean Francois Gravelet ("The Great Blondin")**

The first tightrope walker at Niagara Falls was the Frenchman, Jean Francois Gravelet, better known as Blondin or The Great Blondin. It seems that he got his stage name from his father, who liked to call him "Blondie" when he was a boy. At that time Jean's hair was quite fair.

Blondin's talents on the high wire were apparent at an early age. He performed all over Europe until he came to the United States in 1855. The next four years, he toured the country, sponsored by P. T. Barnum. He was a truly great crowd-pleaser.

Blondin with his manager on his back

He checked out the gorge below the falls in 1858. He wanted to perform across it from Goat Island to the Canadian side, as close to the Horseshoe Fall as possible. At that time, Goat Island was privately owned. Its owners wanted no part of a stunt, saying that such behavior was "dangerous and foolhardy."

Blondin ended up placing his rope further down river, about halfway between the falls and the old Suspension Bridge. The rope was 1300 feet long. To secure it, guys were attached at either end, but the rope still sagged. Its middle was 50 feet lower than the ends. That meant that Blondin would first descend from 175 to 125 feet above the lower river. Then he had to ascend to the other side of the gorge.

A lot of publicity attracted crowds to all of Blondin's performances. His first began at precisely 5:00 P.M., June 30, 1859. Wearing tight-fitting tights, he began a string of greatly successful shows which dazzled audiences that summer. He did just about everything imaginable, such as: laying down on his back; crossing the rope inside a bag, with his arms and legs shackled; cooking an omelet in the middle of the rope and sending it down to the Maid of the Mist boat, after sampling it; doing somersaults; suspending himself by either one leg or arm; walking backwards; riding a bicycle; crossing at night with Roman candles on his balancing pole.

During his third performance, a man named Travis in the Maid of the Mist boat fired a pistol at a hat held by Blondin. That was not an easy thing to do. The boat was not perfectly still in the water.

What was probably the most dangerous and exciting thing Blondin did was carry his manager, Harry Colcord, on his back. They had to rest about 6 times while making the crossing. This meant that poor Harry had to get off Blondin's sweaty back and then climb back up. There were most likely many sweaty hands amongst the onlookers. During one of the three times this stunt was done that season, someone who had wagered against its success cut some of the guy ropes. When Blondin sensed that something was wrong, he hurried to the end of the tightrope. Realizing the danger, many people in the crowds had fainted.

Blondin made most of his money by the "passing of the hat." Onlookers on both sides of the gorge had to pay to watch the performances. The average cost was 25 cents.

Blondin returned in 1860. This time he set up a rope further down the gorge, over the Whirlpool Rapids. During that summer he still managed to amaze his audiences. He wanted to carry the Prince of Wales on his back. The future King Edward VII of England graciously declined the offer. The royal person probably didn't want to end his vacation and life that day.

Blondin was semi-retired for awhile after 1860, but the desire to perform returned. He toured Europe until 1896, when he retired to an estate in England he called "Niagara." There he died in bed in 1897 at the age of 73.

Success breeds imitation. And so it was at Niagara Falls from 1860 until the beginning of the 20th century. Funambulists were there seeking fame and fortune, but none of them was as successful as The Great Blondin.

*"I will lay then a thousand dollars
that I have more people here
than Blondin had."*

— **Signor Guillermo Farini**
(formerly William Leonard Hunt)

Among the crowd watching Blondin perform in 1859 was a Canadian originally from Lockport, New York. His name was William Leonard Hunt, an accomplished circus performer. He thought he could easily surpass Blondin's daring and imagination. In fact, he was so sure of himself that he challenged Blondin to a kind of funambulistic duel, stating,

> "the undersigned challenges M. Blondin as follows: I will carry M. Blondin to the center of the cable across the Niagara River; he to carry me the rest of the distance across. Afterwards to start from each end, proceed to the center and down a rope to the Maid of the Mist returning the same way. I offer this challenge in consequence of M. Blondin's assertion that no man dare perform his feats."

Blondin never replied to the challenge, so Hunt decided to perform in 1860 at the same time as Blondin. The competition between the two proved to be interesting to some spectators, who hurried from one performance to the other. Most of the time, however, Blondin attracted the most attention.

Hunt gave himself another name to possibly compete with his competitor's "European connection." As Signor Guillero Farini, he could become "Farini the Great."

He set up his tightrope near the site of Blondin's first rope. Referring to his situation as, "The Canadian Boy Against the Professional Acrobat," he made every effort to best his French rival.

Farini did just about everything Blondin did, and then some. For example, he once went to the center of his rope, attached a line to it which went down to the Maid of the Mist boat; climbed down to have a chat with the passengers; then climbed back up to his tight-rope. Another time he advertised that he would cross over the gorge on a horse. Well, he did — sort of. He crossed wearing a costume that resembled a horse.

What was most likely Farini's oddest stunt was his portrayal of "Biddy the Irish Washerwoman." No, he didn't wear a dress, but he carried a unique washing machine and clothesline on his back. Over the middle of the gorge, he washed handkerchiefs given to him by some female admirers. Then, with the wash waving in the breeze, he completed his walk.

Overall, Farini made more money than Blondin that summer. They both did their last performances in September. As far as who won the competition, well, history seems to favor the Frenchman.

"Balleni, Balleni, Balleni,
The Great Australian Blondin
is now at Niagara Falls
erecting his monster rope, 1,500 feet long.
The greatest (rope) span ever erected in the world."

Signor Henry Balleni's newspaper advertisement

The American Civil War caused a decrease in tourism at Niagara Falls. The first funambulist of note to perform by the falls after the war was a 32-year-old, Signor Henry Balleni, who was known by many as "The Great Australian Blondin," even though he was born in England and of Italian extraction. His title followed him after he performed well in Australia in 1858.

Balleni and his wife came to Niagara Falls in the summer of 1873. He decided to set his rope up fairly close to the American Fall, from Prospect Park to Canada. The location was quite scenic but much affected by winds created by the large masses of falling water. Balleni was confident that he could master the conditions, just as Blondin and Farini did.

Balleni's 2.25 inch-thick rope was stretched out over 1,420 feet across the gorge. Even though it weighed about 2,500 pounds, many guys were attached to it to keep it steady. Still, it slacked about 80 feet in the middle.

Balleni's first walk on his rope took place in the afternoon of August 25. The rope was too slack. He barely made it up to the American side. Remember, he had to carry his 48-pound balance pole up the rope.

After tightening his tightrope more, Balleni went on to perform many times. He crossed blindfolded; enveloped in a sack; pushing a wheelbarrow. He pretty much did everything Blondin and Farini had done. But he did something his predecessors didn't do. He jumped from the rope.

To help break his fall into the river, he used a 12-foot rubber cord which was attached to the tightrope. On August 25 and 27, everything went well. Balleni jumped and let go of the cord at the right time. On August 31, however, the cord broke as he jumped and wrapped itself around his legs as he entered the water. He was rescued by men in a nearby boat.

He somehow found the water on the 31st to be much colder than on the 27th. That was his reason for announcing that he would not repeat the leap that season. Could the "master" have gotten cold feet from the "cold water?"

After doing other stunts for awhile, Balleni was driven out of town. It seems that one of his assistants, Stephen Peere, a young local Canadian, decided to cross the tightrope one day. When Balleni saw how pleased the crowds were with Peere's stunts, he cut some of the guys. This act enraged Peere's supporters and they turned on the English Italian Blondin.

In the winter of 1885-86, Balleni returned to Niagara Falls. One day, while on the Suspension Bridge, he shook the snow off his shoes, climbed the railing and jumped into the river. He was badly injured and knocked unconscious. That he was rescued again from the *really* cold waters was nearly a miracle.

In 1888, he finally met his match. He died when he jumped from the Hungerford Bridge in London, England.

"Walking across the river
does not display the artiste's nerve
half as much as the different performances
I propose to give on the rope."

Signorina Maria Spelterini

The United States of America celebrated its centennial in 1876. As part of the festivities at Niagara Falls, a 23-year-old Italian woman, Signorina Maria Spelterini, planned to perform on a tightrope on July 4. The heavy rope was set up about 200 feet below the Railway Suspension Bridge (today's Whirlpool Rapids Bridge is on the very same site), where the gorge is about 800 feet wide. It was also the site used by Blondin in 1860.

Because of inclement weather, Signorina Spelterini had to postpone her performance until July 8. It was a sunny, hot and humid day. She seemed at ease out in the open, while spectators desperately tried to keep cool.

Maria was made even prettier by her costume: flesh-colored tights, a scarlet tunic, a sea-green bodice, neat green boots and a large relatively flat hat. She was the first and the last female funambulist at Niagara Falls. Being curious, many people came to see a woman do what a man usually did. After all, those were the so-called Victorian times in Europe and elsewhere. Women were expected to stay home and not do daring things — *especially* in public.

On July 12, Maria walked frontwards and backwards across her cable. She wore the same clothes as on the 8th, but, instead of boots, she wore peach baskets strapped to her feet. On the 19th, she crossed blindfolded. On Saturday, the 22nd, she walked both ways with her wrists and ankles manacled. For her last performance, on Thursday, July 27, she again wore the peach baskets.

"The Signorina," as many affectionately called her, was well-liked by her audiences *and* the people who were staying in the same hotel as she was — the International (now gone). In fact, the hotel guests

Maria over the Whirlpool Rapids, wearing her peach baskets

took up a collection and bought Maria a lovely gold locket. In his presentation speech, Mr. Isaacson, from New Orleans, said:

"Signorina Spelterini:

The lady guests at the International Hotel, whose pleasure it has been to appreciate your many social attractions during your sojourn at Niagara Falls, desire to place in your possession the accompanying token of regard in remembrance of your visit to this noted resort, which doubtless commemorates your 'Crown of Success' in a professional view.

In your departure hence be assured you bear with you the admiration due a woman combining all the virtues of her sex and an artist in whose future welfare and success are fully enlisted the heartfelt sympathy of the Lady Guests."

Maria was quite taken with this gesture and responded in broken English. She left Niagara Falls in an atmosphere of "admiration and delight," according to O. E. Dunlap, a local historian.

*"I will out-do Blondin,
as a Native of Niagara Falls (Ontario),
not by a barrel performance
nor by swimming the whirlpool rapids,
(both had just recently been done)
but by crossing at 3 p.m.
on a five-eighths inch wire cable
a method never before tried."*

Stephen Peer, alias Stephen Peere

The next significant funambulist was a local man, Stephen Peer. He was born in 1840 in Drummondville (now a part of Niagara Falls, Ontario. He was inspired by Blondin's performances over the gorge and spent many years practicing on different kinds of ropes. He started by balancing himself on grapevines twined together and stretched out between trees in his family's orchard. He became even more comfortable with heights by working as a painter.

As already mentioned, he was almost killed by his boss, Henry Balleni, in 1873. That aborted and improvised "performance gave him the incentive to go on to become a professional. And so he did. By 1887, he had become Professor Stephen Peere.

On June 22, he made a grand appearance before his hometown family and friends. His cable was set up over the Whirlpool Rapids, between the Lower Suspension Bridge and Cantilever Bridge (replaced by today's Whirlpool Rapids Bridge and Penn Central Bridge in 1897 and 1925, respectively). He didn't do anything that wasn't done before and he made just a little money by "passing the hat" among the spectators. He seemed pleased with the stunt, but was he?

What happened next is one of Niagara's outstanding mysteries. Stephen Peer died in the evening of June 25, only three days after his gorge crossing. Was he murdered? Did he have an accident? Did he commit suicide?

One story said he fell off his cable while trying to cross it in the dark, wearing hard-soled street shoes. Supposedly, friends dared him to do it. Would he have been so foolish? His descendants don't think so.

In 1971, Peer's niece, and her son, created a memorial to him, The Stephen Peer Memorial Trophy, to be presented, each year, to the winning team of the Greater Niagara Senior Citizens Lawn Bowling Tournament. In a speech made by Peer's great nephew, he said,

> ". . . gamblers and racketeers were making bets that Peer would not make a second walk, and to insure their bets Peer was shot, and his body thrown over the river bank . . ."

One local man related at the time of Peer's death that Peer and some friends had been drinking in a bar and then went out to check the cable. Whether or not the men with Peer were really his friends was only conjectured.

What is known for certain is that Peer's body was found on the rocks about 80 feet down in the gorge. His skull was smashed open, and his brains protruded. He probably died instantly.

"The cable across the Niagara
has been fully tested, and is all right.
As for myself —
well, I'm all right, too."

— Samuel John Dixon

On July 5, 1887, the Canadian Queen Victoria Park Commissioners decided to prohibit tightrope walking along the gorge. This meant that funambulists could not henceforth anchor their ropes or cables on the gorge wall. This decision was a reaction to Peer's death.

Samuel Dixon with the Cantilever Bridge in the background; note the people on the bridge

Despite the prohibition against his "profession," 38-year-old Samuel John Dixon, an American living in Toronto, Canada, was able to get local politicians to get permission for him to perform. After some needed repairs to the cable and its guys, Dixon ended up using Peer's equipment, which had not been taken down.

At exactly 3:30 P.M., on Saturday, September 6, 1890, Dixon stepped upon his sagging slender bridge. He wore terra cotta tights, black silk trunks, a black cap and mocassins. While on the swaying rope, he hung by one leg, lay on his back, and then excited the many spectators when he crossed with his feet encircled by a hoop, which he kept twirling all of the time — first with one foot and then with the other.

After the triumphant reception by his audience, he was interviewed by a local reporter. He made the following statement:

> "The idea of crossing the gorge never occurred to me till a few weeks ago when I was on my way to the Convention of the Photographers' Association of America [his real livelihood was photography, at which he was quite good]. I espied the cable and asked what it was for. I told my informant, a hotel-keeper at Niagara Falls, that I could cross it and he and others who heard my statement scoffed at me. I determined then and there to surprise them."

He returned in 1893 and made relatively uneventful crossings on July 4 and July 13. People were beginning to tire of the funambulists.

"It isn't courage,
a gift of confidence galore."

— Clifford M. Calverly

A long came someone to try to liven things up a bit. His name was Clifford Calverly, a quiet and unassuming young man of 22 from Toronto. He was probably the least egotistical of Niagara's funambulists.

He set up his cable in the same location as Peer's and Dixon's. It was a little thicker than theirs. Hoping to attract a good crowd, he advertised his intentions and spoke to the press. He seemed to impress the Buffalo Express. It reported:

> "the climax of this record-lowering season is promised by Mr. — or probably it is Professor — Clifford Calverly, who will not only try to walk across Niagara gorge on a wire cable, a thing which others have repeatedly done, but will undertake by a display of rapid walking to lower the Blondin-Dixon records by several minutes!"

*Clifford Calverly crossing the gorge over the Whirlpool
Rapids; notice the people on the suspension bridge and at
the top of the gorge*

The Daily Cataract of the young city of Niagara Falls, New York,
was not as impressed, saying:

> "neither Blondin nor Dixon, nor Stephen Peere, did
> their Niagara wire acts against time. These artists were
> content to get across at all, or saw greater art and more
> honor in dallying by the way and cutting up moonshines
> 200 feet above the water."

His first walk took place at 3:10 P.M., on Wednesday, October
12, 1892. It was an international affair. Canadian and American flags
waved in the wind on both sides of the border and at the ends of
Calverly's balance pole.

He ran across his cable, did all kinds of gymnastics, and then
walked out wearing peachbaskets, which he then kicked off. On an-

other trip on his cable, he took a chair out with him, sat on it, took out a newspaper and read it while enjoying a cigarette. Then he startled his audience by shooting forward from the chair and falling from the cable and saving himself from certain death by catching it with his toes.

He returned the following year and was able to delight the crowds. On July 4, he set a record for the fastest crossing, a mere two minutes and 32.4 seconds. Needless to say, he was quite out of breath when he reached the other side. That evening, he created another spectacle by setting off Roman candles and other kinds of fireworks as he walked across.

He continued to perform as a funambulist for a number of years and then retired to Sarasota, Florida, after working as a bank president.

In 1941, he visited the falls and told reporters that he would like to cross the gorge again in 1942, on the 50th anniversary of his first performance. He was in excellent health for a man of 73. He never did it. Officials on both sides of the Niagara River would not allow it.

"I know these people [the police]
do not give out permits to commit suicide,
but I am a professional
and I believe I have proved it."

— **Henri Julien Rechatin**

The era of funambulism had ended near the turn of the century. Going over the falls in barrels and whatnot came into vogue. Once and awhile someone would make an effort to obtain permission to perform on a rope or cable stretched out across the beautiful gorge, but both Canadian and American authorities have remained adamantly against such "foolishness." It's much easier to violate the letter of the law by hurrying into something and then floating over the falls. Setting up tightropes isn't something that can be done quickly or covertly.

And so, the 20th century funambulist is left with but one choice at Niagara Falls. Cross on something already there. A bridge would not require much skill. Anyone can do that. What's left? A little over 2.5 miles north of the falls is an amusement over the Whirlpool known as the Spanish Aerial Car or Spanish Aero Car.

The aerial or aero car crosses the spinning abyss on sturdy cables, going from one point in Canada to the other. Unlike a regular funambulist's cable or rope, the cables over the Whirlpool are not held securely by guys, so wind is a serious problem. To make matters even worse, they are also greased.

So it seems that no person would attempt a trip across slippery swiping tightropes. Wrong. In 1975, not one, but three people did it together, using a marvelously contrived contraption.

On Wednesday, June 4, at about 6:45 A.M., Henri Julien Rechatin, his wife Janyck and his friend, Frank Lucas took the dangerous trip ever taken across the Niagara River gorge. Lucas, a French motocross champion, drove a motorcycle on the cable. Attached to the machine were two perches, one above it and one below it. On the upper perch stood Henri, holding his balance pole. He had to keep everyone and everything upright. On the lower perch was Janyck, hanging from one foot.

As soon as the trio started their stunt, something went terribly wrong. The cycle could not go on. There was a bump in the cable, a place where two sections were connected. Henri kept his cool and carefully got down and lifted each wheel of the cycle over the bump.

When about halfway across, the long (1800 feet) cable began to sway a lot. Lucas was not too sure of himself. After all, this was the first time he did such a stunt. Henri sensed a problem, so he got down and walked with Lucas the rest of the way. Janyck, meanwhile, climbed onto her perched and wished she was back in France with her children.

After more problems getting by the Aero car parked near the other end of the cable, the trio made landfall. There they were "welcomed" by the authorities.

In 1995, Henri wanted to celebrate the 20th anniversary of his stunt by repeating it. At 63, he was still quite agile. He couldn't get permission to do it. That he didn't do it anyway could be a sign of the wisdom that usually comes with age.

"I am not a stuntman.
I am not a daredevil.
I am an artiste.
Each time I walk I put my life on the wire.
I hope to give the greatest gift
that a high-wire walker can give
to die on my wire."

— **Philippe Petit**

In the summer of 1973, the famous French funambulist, Philippe Petit, walked more than 1,000 feet between the towers of the World Trade Center in New York City. His cable was about 1,350 feet above the ground. After completing the stunt, he was arrested and given a psychiatric examination. He passed it.

Shortly thereafter, he went to Niagara Falls to check it out for a walk. His conclusion? "In the world of the possible, walking across the swirling, spewing, foaming falls is just this side of impossible."

In March of 1976, he returned to the falls and checked into a local inn by the American Rapids. He did a lot of research about the area at the Schoellkopf Geological Museum, the Local History Department of the Earl W. Bridges Library and other places. He explored the gorge by the falls, despite the dangerous ice mounds and possibility of falling rocks. He wanted to be well prepared, should he be given permission to perform.

"To me it is like a detective story," he said. "I must find all those clues and solve all those problems: how to prevent rocks from falling, where to put my guy wires and towers, how to learn the winds and mists and every other thing. I've been thinking of walking above Niagara Falls for about 10 years. I've been compiling things for a long time but have become very serious about it only in the past year.

It is not talent I have but intensity, an inside fire, a taste of perfection. I feel I belong to the sky. It is the moment of purest happiness." Then, referring to a walk by the falls, he said, "this will be done, because I want it . . . I love anything gigantic."

Well, he didn't do it. He could not get permission from Canadian and American park officials. They said the stunt would be too dangerous for spectators and Petit's performance might encourage copycats.

In October of 1986, Petit did get to "pretend" crossing the Niagara gorge. Actually, he walked on a wire about 45 feet long over the river bank at Table Rock, close to the Horseshoe Fall. He was hired to recreate Blondin's first 1859 walk across the gorge. The re-enactment was part of a film being prepared for a theater in Canada.

Daring The Lower Rapids

Nearly all stunts performed below the falls were done in the latter part of the nineteenth century and the first three decades of the twentieth century. A few men swam through the Whirlpool Rapids. Both men and women rode inside barrels and in boats through the same waters. Some of the daredevils paid the ultimate price for their foolhardiness.

Those who rode in barrels and boats will be called "Rapidriders." For nearly all of them, the Whirlpool became a spinning trap from which a rescue could take many hours.

It must be noted that when these stunts took place much more water passed through the lower rapids. Starting in the 1950's, the amount of water has dropped between 50 and 75 percent.

*"It's the angriest bit of water
in the world, I've been told,
but I know I can do it.
I'm going all the way down
and through the Whirlpool, to Lewiston."*

— **Captain Matthew Webb**

On August 24, 1875, Matthew Webb became the first person, as far as it is known, to swim across the English Channel, from Dover to Calais, about 25 miles. He was just 27 years old, but having served on ships since the age of 12 made him strong and mature. He came to the United States in 1882, not realizing he was leaving his home in England forever. He toured that country and Canada, winning swimming meets and becoming famous for accomplishments in water. While in Toronto, he bragged about plans to swim the rapids below Niagara Falls.

After an offer of 10,000 dollars from railway owners who hoped to gain from the attraction of a stunt below the falls, Webb came to the falls in July of 1883. He announced his plans to challenge the rapids and Whirlpool, telling the press,

"I don't intend to have any problem swimming the rapids. I'll dive and swim under them when I run into trouble — not over them."

And so, in the afternoon of July 24, he went down the road to the Canadian Maid of the Mist landing. There a boat took him out into the middle of the river and headed for the lower rapids. At about 4:25 P.M., after the ferryman begged him to change his mind, Webb, wearing the red cotton swimming trunks he had worn when he crossed the English Channel, dove into the 39-mile-per-hour water.

He was seen riding the top of the huge waves until he neared the old railroad bridge. Then he disappeared. It wasn't until four days later that a local American resident found Webb's body near the Lewiston Landing. There was a three-inch gash in his head, which probably was caused by striking a rock. He died from a fractured skull, not by drowning.

He was buried in Oakwood Cemetery, in Niagara Falls, New York. His wife and children never received a cent from the railway owners, and she could not sue because there was no written contract.

On Tuesday, August 24, 1886, a young man from Lewiston, New York, decided he could swim the lower rapids. He wore a pair of rubber trunks and a cork life-preserver. He didn't make it. His body was taken out of the river the same day.

"He did nothing in his cask except hold on and get sick, and possibly think of himself for a moment as the fool he certainly was."

— *The Spectator*, July 17, 1886, commenting on Carlisle D. Graham's trip through the Whirlpool Rapids in a barrel

Carlisle D. Graham, originally from England, came to Niagara Falls from Philadelphia in July of 1886. A cooper (barrel builder) by trade, he thought he'd ride in one of his own making through the Whirlpool Rapids. This would be the first barrel stunt of any kind by the falls.

Despite warnings from many people, Graham was determined to go through with his trip. To be safe, he first sent some identical barrels through the rapids. Each one contained sand equivalent in weight to his-own. They all made it undamaged.

On Sunday afternoon, July 11, his barrel was towed out to a point just south of the cantilever bridge (near the site of today's rusting railroad bridge). He got inside and fitted himself into a cloth sack attached to the inside of the barrel. His hands passed through holes so he could hold on to iron handles. To keep upright, he ballasted one end of the barrel. Air could enter through a small hole.

The barrel was released and soon became totally at the mercy of the quick current and violent waves. It turned over and over, over and over. It went around and around, around and around. Graham held on for dear life as water came in through his air hole. Fortunately, he didn't get too wet, because the sack was waterproof. He did get sick and dizzy, quite sick and dizzy.

After about 5 minutes in the rapids, he entered the calmer waters of the Whirlpool. There he went around and around for awhile. Then he entered the Devil's Hole Rapids and was bounced around a little more. Finally, after about 30 minutes in transit, he reached his destination — Lewiston.

Something must have happened to his balance. Soon he declared his intention of repeating the trip, but with his head sticking out of the barrel. He seemed determined to kill himself.

On August 19 of the same year, he did it. Yes, he did it. Picture this. A man's head sticking out of a barrel as it bobbed and bounced through what was probably the-most dangerous rapids in the world. Waves kept striking the sides of Graham's head.

He survived, but for the rest of his life he was hard of hearing, literally.

Carlisle D. Graham standing proudly by the barrel he rode in through the Whirlpool Rapids, the Whirlpool and the Devil's Hole Rapids

*"Among those who were inspired
to sink or swim in the Niagara
as a result of having been shown how
by Carlisle D. Graham
were William Potts and George Hazlett."*

— **Orrin E. Dunlap**

George Hazlett and William Potts were two men from Buffalo, New York, who decided to be the first duet rapidriders at Niagara. They built a barrel totally unique from all wooden barrels ever used for stunting over or below the falls. It was about ten feet long and made of oak staves 1.75 inches thick. The inside was divided into three compartments. Four feet from the smaller "front" end were two bulkheads protected by a sheet of iron. The larger compartment was for the "crew."

Unlike Graham's, this barrel was meant to float on its side. To make that possible, a keel made of thick oak was attached. To assist in moving about in calm water, an iron rudder was added to the "stern." It could be controlled from inside. On "top" of the barrel there was a small round projection with very small windows. The craft was decorated with a small American flag.

After advertising their intentions, a good-sized crowd gathered to see the stunt. It took place on Sunday, August 8, 1886. The captain of the new Maid of the Mist boat wanted no part of such foolishness, so Potts and Hazlett hired the crew of a small boat to tow the barrel out to the head of the Whirlpool Rapids. At 4:55 P.M., the rapidriders were cut loose and began their death-defying journey. They were tossed about like a toy in a bathtub by a rowdy child. The rapids had no idea which part of the barrel was the top or bottom, stern or bow. Through it all, however, the flag blew in the wind and was never lost.

After one trip around the Whirlpool, the barrel went through the rest of the rapids and ended up in Lewiston. There, friends of the rapidriders caught it and safely brought its crew to shore. Potts and Hazlett were quite shaken up and somewhat bruised. Someone overheard them say their next trip might be over the falls.

"I think we ought to come to Niagara and do something desperate to make a reputation."

— **Carlisle D. Graham**

Carlisle Graham's third trip through the lower rapids took place on June 15, 1887. He used a new and longer barrel, so he could stand upright. He first advertised that he would be on the outside of the barrel throughout the stunt. Yes, the outside. Then he changed his mind. He realized that to do so would probably guarantee a painful demise.

The crowds which had gathered that day expected to see a stunt, so Graham figured he'd better do something. Around 5 P.M., he climbed into his craft and secured his feet between the sandbags at the "bottom." He braced himself against the staves, as the barrel was released just above the Whirlpool Rapids.

The trip through those rapids took about 3 minutes. To many onlookers, the barrel resembled a cork bouncing in rough waters. It entered the great Whirlpool and proceeded to go around and around for what seemed an eternity, but was really just about 23 minutes.

Fearing Graham was dead, some people began to try and get his attention by firing guns. Being hard of hearing, he probably heard nothing. Then someone threw a stone which struck the bobbing barrel. Suddenly, out popped Graham's head, much like a jack-in-the-box. After looking around a bit, he dove into the perilous water and swam to the shore. Later, despite many bruises, he swam back to his primitive conveyance and brought it back to the shore.

He challenged the rapids again in 1889 and 1901. Then in 1905, he challenged a younger man, William J. Clover, to a swimming con-

*Carlisle Graham (far left) and William Glover on his right,
just before the swimming contest*

test in the Whirlpool Rapids. And so, on Monday, July 17, 1905, the
two daredevils, entered the water, not at all certain of the outcome.
At stake, besides their lives, were a $200 purse and a side bet of
$1,000. After nearly drowning in an eddy, Graham lost the race. That
pretty much ended his career as a Niagara challenger.

Graham lived the rest of his life in Niagara Falls, New York. He is
buried near Annie Taylor.

"I'm going to swim to Canada."

— **William J. Kendall**

In August of 1886, William J. Kendall, 24, supposedly a former Boston, Massachusetts, policeman, came to Niagara Falls to swim through the Whirlpool Rapids. He was warned by many local residents not to try it, but he was determined to win a wager of $1,000 that he could do it.

On Sunday afternoon, August 22, he went down to the Maid of the Mist landing on the Canadian side of the river. Wearing only a bathing suit and cork life preserver, he dove into the water, shouting to a group of boys nearby, "I'm going to Canada." Why did he say that? After all, he was staying in Canada.

He started his stunt at exactly 2:00. No sooner did he reach the middle of the river, he was caught by a countercurrent. When he realized he was going in the wrong direction, he searched for and found the main current and was on his way to the Whirlpool. At 2:05, he entered the rapids and was soon seen struggling to keep his head above water. The huge waves tossed him about badly. Some spectators thought he would share Captain Webb's fate.

Just as he entered the Whirlpool, his body was thrown nearly 10 feet and then went underwater, only to resurface 100 feet toward the center of the eddy. There the current took him to the center, where he was sucked under. Lucky for him, the river threw him out only seconds later. It was possible to be held under for hours, or even *days.*

Dazed and weak, he struggled with all his might to swim for the shore. He made it to a rock and held on to it to rest. Then he was rescued. Except for a few minor bruises, he was alright.

Later that day, after going to the American side of the river, he told a reporter:

> "there isn't enough money in the world to hire me to make the trip again. While going through the rapids, I was tossed and tumbled until I knew not where I was. The weight of the waves was terrible and I was pounded until I am sore all over. I knew nothing while going through, though I realized that I turned three complete somersaults. When I entered the Whirlpool I was in good condition, but spinning around like a top and being drawn under. I lost consciousness then for a short time. The whirl made me terribly sick. I threw myself on my back and pushed for shore. Go through again? No, sir. I made the swim for money there was in it, but I won't do it again."

William Kendall wearing his cork life preserver

"Come, George, I'm all fixed."

— Sadie Allen to George Hazlett as they were
about to enter their barrel

George Hazlett was really turned on by his ride through the Whirlpool Rapids. Somehow he talked a young woman, only 17 years-old, to go along with him for a repeat performance. Her name was Sadie Allen. She was petite and her demeanor in no way appeared daring. George bet her $5 that she would scream during their trip.

And so, at about 2:30 P.M., on an unusually mild November 28, 1886, the pair of rapidriders left the Maid of the Mist dock on the Canadian side of the lower river. Their barrel, the very same one Hazlett shared with Potts on August 8, was towed by a boat owned by a man known as "Slippery Joe." Huge crowds were gathered everywhere, even on the bridges.

The trip through the Whirlpool only took a few minutes. As expected, the barrel had been bounced around and went up and down, over and around. After floating around the Whirlpool for about 45 minutes, a rope was successfully thrown to the barrel from the Canadian shore. Hazlett, who had gone part of the way out of the hatch, caught the rope and held on to it as rescuers pulled the barrel to the shore.

Both George and Sadie were badly bruised. It was also obvious that Sadie had vomited while passing through the rapids. She did win the bet, however.

A local newspaper later announced that "Hazlett and Miss Allen will go on exhibition in some museum." Not a bad idea, although a circus sideshow might be a better idea.

*"I would not hesitate to repeat my trip
every day. It amounts to nothing
in such a boat as I have built,
and is just as safe as though you were in a
life boat on an open sea during a storm."*

— **Charles Alexander Percy**

C harles Percy was a wagon maker and a well known resident of the village called Suspension Bridge (because of the bridge of that type crossing the gorge nearby; that village is now the north side of the City of Niagara Falls, New York). He spent his spare time constructing a special boat. According to him, his desire was,

> "to devise a lifeboat that in a time of danger can be thrown overboard from the deck of a vessel or steamer without the use of davits, and that will right itself as soon as it strikes the water."

Perhaps Percy's idea should have been investigated by the builders of the infamous Titanic. Who knows?

His boat was very well made. It was 17 feet long and about five feet wide. He covered it with waterproof canvas. On either side of a four-foot square chamber were two air-tight chambers. The middle chamber had a seat for one occupant who could either ride in the open air or with the hatch closed. Two long oars could be strapped to the boat when not in use. To keep the boat upright its keel was made of iron and a dozen sandbags were scattered about inside. To prevent the craft from spinning around in the rapids, a 30-pound iron weight was used as a drag from the stern.

Unannounced, Percy's trip took place on September 28, 1887. He began it below the falls at about 3:15 P.M. He made it through the Whirlpool Rapids, but the drag didn't work. He spun around many times. The boat did not turn over, however.

He entered the Whirlpool at 3:40. He made it to the shore unassisted. Later, he told reporters about the trip.

"After I had gone into the air chamber, when those first billows were struck, the sensation was like that experienced in riding into a heavy sea, and when I struck the breaker that rushes out from the shore near Brundage's incline railway, the little boat keeled most fearfully. She did not rock much, but when she did rock, it was something awful. At one time she got a fearful slap from the waves, and I imagined that I was knocked about a hundred feet through the air, striking the water with such force that I felt certain a hole had been knocked in her side. There was some water in the air chamber when I started. We put it in to cool off the place. This was thrown over me and made me think that an accident had occurred. When the waves were crested I got it the worst. I did not mind my experience in the whirlpool as I was not in the most violent part of it." Percy later said he would probably never make the trip again. He said he didn't do it for fame or fortune, but just to test the reliability of his boat. Well, like so many of his kind, he did do it again, 15 years later, on September 7, 1902.

"Articles of agreement made and concluded
this 21st day of June, 1888, between Charles
Alexander Percy of Suspension Bridge, N.Y.,
and Robert William Flack of Syracuse, N.Y.
It is hereby agreed that, whereas Charles
Alexander Percy has issued a challenge
to said William Flack to row a race through what
is known as Whirlpool Rapids to what is known as

> *the public dock at Lewiston, N.Y., and such*
> *challenge issued by Percy has been accepted by*
> *said Flack, that within six weeks from this date*
> *that Charles Alexander Percy and Robert William*
> *Flack meet on some day to be hereinafter agreed*
> *upon, at the Maid of the mist landing prepared to*
> *row the race. It is understood the race is to be*
> *for $500 a side."*

— **Articles of agreement signed by Percy and Flack**

Robert William Flack, 39, came to Niagara Falls in the summer of 1888 with a boat he made for a possible trip through the rapids in the gorge. He met with Charles Percy and they soon decided to have a contest, a race from the Canadian Maid of the Mist landing to Lewiston. They drew up the agreement shown above.

Flack wanted to test his craft before the race, so he chose the 4th of July, a time when huge crowds usually gathered at the falls. He advertised his intentions. This resulted in a mass of people all along the gorge and on the bridges.

He began from the landing at about 3 P.M., strapped to his seat. After he was about midway through the Whirlpool Rapids, the boat capsized, but then immediately righted itself. The last wave of that rapids catapulted the boat end over end into the Whirlpool. It landed upside down and stayed that way for about an hour, as rescuers tried in vain to get it.

Charles Percy arrived on the scene and hurried to the shore and dove into the Whirlpool, shouting, "I'll catch it or die."

He swam out to the boat as it neared the shore and pulled it in, all the while hoping he wasn't too late. As soon as possible, the boat was turned over and Flack was quite dead, still strapped to his harness. The race would never occur.

Flack's body was returned to his family in Syracuse, but it was buried in Toronto, Ontario, his original home. (He settled there after emigrating from England.)

By the way, Flack had a manager who was an undertaker.

*"I am on my holidays,
and I thought that to make this trip
would be more exciting
than to lie in the shade fishing."*

— **Peter Nissen, alias F. M. Bowser**

eter Nissen, an accountant from Chicago, came to Niagara Falls in June of 1900 with a boat and a dream. His boat, his own creation, was quite unusual. It was about 20 feet long and 4 feet deep and its beam (extreme width) was 6 feet. To keep it upright, it had an iron keel weighing about 1,250 pounds. The deck was completely covered except for a small cockpit at its center. There were also air compartments fore and aft, as well as on either side of the cockpit.

Flack seated in the boat he called the "Phantom."

Nissen hoped to prove that his "Fool Killer" was fit to be used by tourists who desired to ride the rapids below the falls. He wanted to open such a dangerous attraction in the near future. Perhaps there might someday be a fleet of "Fool Killers."

Luck was not with Peter, at first. Delay after delay frustrated his audiences. Finally, on a stormy July 9, "F. M. Bowser," his stage name, had his creation towed to the head of the Whirlpool Rapids. After another delay, he began his test ride about 5 P.M.

After a bumpy trip through the great waves, he ended up spending over an hour going around and around the Whirlpool. When Fool Killer came close enough to the shore, it was retrieved.

Describing his experience, Nissen said,

> "I waved my hand to someone at the elevator on the Canadian side, and just then a wave struck me full in the face. It hit me an awful blow, like a hammer, and seemingly I was under water. My lungs filled twice, and I had to cough hard. I did not lose consciousness, however. When I came up again I watched the waves, and prepared myself for them by drawing long breaths and ducking my head as I met them. I never suffered after that, but they hit me so hard that I was afraid they would break my neck. The rapids were worse than I thought them."

The next day, Peter finished his trip to Lewiston. His boat lost a rudder and iron keel. He decided he had to go back to his "drawing boards."

He returned in 1901 with a new "Fool Killer." It was a foot longer and 2 feet narrower than its predecessor. It also had an eight-horsepower steam engine. After some test runs in the calmer waters north of the lower rapids, Nissen rode the rapids on October 12. His rapid ride was filmed by the one and only Thomas A. Edison, who shot the film in the gorge while on a streetcar owned by the Great Gorge Route company.

The next day, Nissen and a friend rode the boat together through the rapids into the Whirlpool, where they wanted to make depth soundings. Well, the boat was severely damaged by driftwood, and the two men jumped to the American shore when they had the chance. Fool Killer later sank in the Whirlpool.

Nissen never saw his dream come true. He did, however, suggest that there might be a lot of gold at the bottom of the Whirlpool. With all that water going around all the time, by now all lighter materials

Peter Nissen's boat "Fool Killer" by the shore of the Whirlpool

would have been washed away, or so he thought. Some say he spent too much time going around the Whirlpool.

"Fake!"

— Shouted by some spectators when Martha E. Wagenfuhrer refused to go into her damaged barrel

Martha E. Wagenfuhrer was a brave young woman from Buffalo, New York. She was hoping to win fame and fortune by riding in a barrel through the Whirlpool Rapids, the first woman to do so. She and her manager decided to do it on the same day President William McKinley was planning to come to the falls from the Pan-American Exposition in Buffalo — Saturday, September 6, 1901. By the way, later that day, the president was assassinated in Buffalo.

Calling herself, the "Maid of the Niagara Falls Rapids," Martha advertised that her ride would begin at 2:30 P.M. Despite a waning interest in daredevils at Niagara Falls, a few thousand people lined the gorge and packed the electric cars of the Great Gorge Route.

Her stunt was delayed when the barrel accidentally rolled down the bank of the lower river and was damaged. Martha absolutely refused to go on until the damage was repaired. Many spectators didn't like the delay, calling her a "fake."

Finally, at 5:45 P.M., the rapidrider began to make history. The "maid" was strapped well inside her barrel, but the rough ride must have been too much for her. After going around the Whirlpool for over an hour, she was rescued and found unconscious. It took over ten minutes to restore her. Otherwise, she was uninjured.

Meanwhile, her manager had taken up a collection to buy her a diamond emblem. He was able to gather a large sum.

Martha E. Wagenfuhrer, the "maid of Niagara Falls Rapids"

"Now and then the tossing barrel could be seen, tumbling and rolling about on the waves and current."

— **Description of Maud Willard's barrel trapped for many hours in the Whirlpool in *Current Literature*, March, 1901**

Carlisle Graham, the successful five-time rapidrider, decided to team up with a young burlesque performer, Maud Willard, to do a double stunt in the Niagara River gorge. Maud was to ride in the barrel used by her friend, Martha Wagenfuhrer, through the Whirlpool Rapids and into the Whirlpool. As soon as Maud would be rescued, Graham was to dive into the pool from the American side and swim through the Devil's Hole Rapids to Lewiston.

The double stunt took place on Sunday, September 7, 1901, the day after Martha Wagenfuhrer's successful rapidride. At 3:53 P.M., the barrel containing Maud and her pet fox terrier was towed out into the middle of the lower river and released above the Whirlpool Rapids. The trip through the white water was the usual bumpy experience.

When the barrel entered the Whirlpool, it went to the center. That was *not* the best place to end up. After going around and around for awhile, it was sucked under by a deep whirl. Then it popped up more than a hundred feet from where it disappeared. It kept drifting too far from rescuers. It also had a pronounced list, something not observed before.

Graham watched his partner's plight for quite some time. He knew that his agreement with Maud said that he should go on with his part if the barrel's retrieval was delayed, and so he did. His swim was filmed by a moving-picture machine.

*Carlisle Graham and Maul Willard standing on either side of
the ill-fated barrel*

After completing his part, Graham hurried back to the Whirlpool — this time he stood at the top of the gorge. He was saddened to
see Maud's barrel still in a perilous predicament.

Soon darkness came. Bonfires were set on the Canadian shore,
their light casting an eerie glow on the mysterious huge eddy. Then a
searchlight car from the Great Gorge Route parked on the American
side and cast its lights on the water. Every once and awhile the tossing and bobbing wooden craft could be seen.

By 9 P.M., Maud and her dog had been in the barrel over five hours. By 9:20, the barrel finally came close enough to the shore to be retrieved. When the hatch was removed, the terrier jumped out playfully. Inside, however, Maud's body was limp and lifeless. She had suffocated.

The barrel had one air hole. Apparently, the dog must have stuck its nose into the hole, depriving its owner of air. That pooch was obviously not womans' best friend.

"My principal reason in making the trip
is for the purpose of having exclusive
moving pictures made."

— **William "Red" Hill Sr.**

Probably the most famous riverman who ever lived by Niagara Falls was William "Red" Hill, a resident of Niagara Falls, Ontario. Through much of the first half of the 20th century, he saved many lives in the treacherous waters above and below the falls. He also assisted authorities in retrieving bodies in the gorge hundreds of times.

Red was also a daredevil. In 1901, he rode Bobby Leach's barrel through the Whirlpool Rapids. On May 30, 1930, Memorial Day, he rode in a steel barrel of his own making through all the rapids below the falls, from the Canadian Maid of the Mist landing to Queenston. His trip was smooth and uneventful. He took the ride lying in a hammock.

In 1931, he repeated his trip, but this time he used the ill-fated barrel used by the late George Stathakis. By the way, he didn't take Stathakis' turtle along for the ride.

William "Red" Hill Sr. in his steel cask

*"That's the biggest, meanest river I ever saw.
It doesn't look as bad as it really is."*

— **Jim Sarten**

On Thursday afternoon, July 4, 1974, Jim Sarten, 37, an experienced stuntman, shot the Whirlpool Rapids sitting on a raft made of wood and oil drums. He wore a wetsuit jacket and life jacket. He also had a small scuba diving oxygen tank. He did the stunt as a part of the production of the movie "The Mighty Niagara," The film company, Playboy Productions, had dummies which could have been used instead of a real person.

While passing through the rapids, Sarten found it difficult to breath at times, later saying, "you exhale and get slapped by water coming in your mouth."

To help him with the problem, he decided to keep his head underwater as much as possible and make use of the oxygen tank. All he had to do was make it to the Whirlpool, where a safety boat was waiting. Then something terrible happened,

Somehow, he was knocked out. His body, floating face down, was taken from the Whirlpool. When all efforts to revive him seemed useless, he suddenly came to, coughing up large amounts of water. He also had bruises and a concussion.

Once he felt better, Sarten told a reporter,

> "I sort of enjoyed it. I was breathing okay. I knew I was travelling very, very fast and it was just a matter of minutes before I'd reach the safety boat. I understand the water. It's not going to tear my limbs or suck my skin off. I do this all the time and I get water in my lungs all the time."

Sarten said rapids were rated on a scale of one to ten, ten being the roughest. What did he rate the Whirlpool Rapids? An eleven! He should have known. He was no dummy.

"The Niagara River is too tough for any raft."

— George Butterfield, one of the people who saw
a raft carrying 30 passengers capsize in the
Whirlpool Rapids

That the average person could be a daredevil at Niagara Falls had been Peter Nissen's unfulfilled dream, back in 1900. The lure of Niagara's falls and rapids has been an exciting and sometimes frightening part of the Niagara experience. People often feel drawn to the water. There have been cases where a man or woman will suddenly find themselves in the rapids, not remembering how it happened.

In 1975, the Niagara Gorge River Trips, Inc., offered anyone the chance to ride a raft on the Whirlpool Rapids. The maiden voyage of the one-ton nylon and neoprene "completely safe" floater took place in the afternoon of August 29. On it were a crew of two and 27 passengers.

There was a lot of excitement among the rapidriders as they entered the Whirlpool Rapids. Everything went well until the raft struck a 20-foot wave, went up in the air and flipped over, like a flapjack. There was a desperate struggle to get to the shore. Twenty-four made it alive, while three others drowned when trapped under the heavy raft.

The raft, called the Grider, was built by people who misjudged the element on which it was to travel, much like the builders of the ill-fated Titanic.

You Name It
And Someone
Probably Did It

This last chapter is about interesting and unique stunts performed by Niagara's challengers. That it takes all kinds of people to make the world go around has been exemplified very well at Niagara Falls.

Women seldom do crazy or unusual things at Niagara. Perhaps someone can explain why men have a propensity for dangerous behavior. Whatever the reason or reasons, such behavior peaked during the latter part of the last century and the first few decades of this century.

Imagine a man trying to "walk" on the river below the falls. Also imagine a man flying a biplane under the steel arch of a bridge spanning the gorge. He did it *with his eyes closed*! Then imagine a man trying to wade across the American Rapids. Can these stunts be topped? You bet. Imagine a man trying to cross the gorge with his teeth holding on to a pulley attached to a rope.

*"Some things can be done
as well as others."*

— Sam Patch

Who was Sam Patch? Well, the answer depends on who is asked. After his many jumps in the 1820's, he became a folk hero to many Americans. He became a symbol of speed and power. His antics were imitated by men and woman. According to Elizabeth McKinsey, author of the excellent book, *Niagara Falls, Icon of the American Sublime,* 1985, Patch "challenged Niagara gratuitously, simply for the sake of the challenge."

In 1881, William Purcell, editor of the Rochester Union and Advertiser, had a much different impression of Patch, saying,

> "Sam Patch was a man of weak mind, fond of strong drink, who resorted to the original device of jumping from great heights to attract attention."

A depiction of Sam Patch on his platform waving to the crowds

One thing about Sam Patch about which people do agree is that he was Niagara's first real daredevil. He also inspired later people to challenge the falls and their river.

He was born around 1807 on a Massachusetts farm. He became a spinner in a cotton mill which stood by the top of the Pawtucket

Falls. Like other young men, he enjoyed jumping into the water below the falls. Jumping turned him on, and he liked the attention it got him.

Patch decided to pursue a career in jumping. Why not? He was good at it. His popularity mushroomed in September of 1827, when he jumped into the Passaic Falls in New Jersey. His huge audience thought he was the greatest performer of all time.

According to the Rochester Democrat and Chronicle of Sunday, November 8, 1987, "Patch was probably born modest, but it wore off." Indeed, it did.

In 1829, to help improve the tourist trade, a group of hotel keepers in Niagara Falls, New York, advertised that Patch would jump into the falls. During the first week of October, Patch erected his platform in the gorge below Goat Island, by the Cave of the Winds. The platform was at the top of two 96-foot ladders stretched out 85 feet over the plunge pool of the BriVeil Fall. Guys attached to rocks in the wall of the gorge held the ladders in place.

On Wednesday, October 7, in a pouring rain, Sam climbed to his platform. Just before his stunt, he waved to the crowds. Then he dove into the abyss. A minute or two passed. Some in the audience sighed with despair. Then, all of a sudden, Sam appeared and swam to the shore. Cheers echoed in the chasm, nearly drowning out the thunder of the falls.

A local Canadian paper described Patch's stunt, saying,

"The celebrated Sam Patch actually leaped over the falls of Niagara into the abyss below on the seventh instant. A ladder was projected 40 feet down on which Sam walked out; clad in white with great deliberation put his hands to his sides and jumped from the platform. While the boats below were on the lookout for him, he had, in one minute, reached the shore unnoticed and unhurt and was heard singing merrily on the beach."

All fired up with success, Sam decided to repeat his performance, but with the platform 130 feet above the water. And so, on Saturday, October 17, at exactly 3 P.M., he did it.

He became famous throughout the world. He didn't, however, make very much money. Not many of the crowds of onlookers paid to see the two performances. The hotel keepers on both sides of the Niagara River made out like bandits.

Two months later, on November 13, 1829, Patch jumped into the Genesee Falls in Rochester, New York. Thousands of people came from miles around to see the great entertainer. Patch gave the following immodest speech just before jumping:

> "Napoleon was a great man and a great general. He conquered armies, and he conquered nations, but he couldn't jump the Genesee Falls. Wellington was a great man and a great soldier. He conquered armies and he conquered Napoleon, but he couldn't jump the Genesee Falls. That was left for me to do, and I can do it, and I will."

He could do it. He did do it. He didn't conquer it. It conquered him. He died.

"If we don't see you before then, Mr. Peer, good-bye."

— Comment in a local paper after Henry Peer announced his intentions to leap from the Upper Suspension Bridge into the gorge

Henry P. Peer, cousin of the funambulist, Steve Peer, came to Niagara Falls from Elmira, New York, in the spring of 1879. Unlike his cousin, Steve was not planning to perform on a wire. He planned to perform connected to a wire.

Henry placed a small wooden platform outside the railing at the middle of the Upper Suspension Bridge. Above the platform, he attached a cylinder to the railing. Inside the cylinder about 220 feet of brass wire was wound.

Peer planned to fall from the platform with the brass wire attached to a harness on his back. The wire was supposed to keep his fall perpendicular to the river.

On Wednesday, May 21, with a steady wind blowing, he got on the platform a little after 3 P.M. Besides tights, he wore an inflated life preserver, an elastic band around his legs (to keep them from spreading when he fell) and sponges in his mouth, nostrils and ears.

After saying "good-bye" to people near to him, Henry lower himself at the end of the platform, holding on with his hands. At 3:40, he let go, put his arms at his sides and fell straight down the 200 feet to the river. He went under for a few seconds and then popped up. He was picked up by the rescue boat and taken to the shore. His life preserver burst upon impact with the water. Henry was quite alright.

Shortly after his successful plunge, he said that he would do it again on July 4. He showed up that day, intoxicated, but chickened out. He never fell again, at least not into the Niagara River.

"Tell me if there is anything higher [than Niagara Falls] that Larry could jump off of?"

— **The question asked of a reporter by Larry Donovan's mother**

L awrence M. Donovan was a young man who liked to jump. He became famous after jumping from the Brooklyn Bridge. He came to Niagara Falls in October of 1886 and announced that he was going to jump from the Upper Suspension Bridge.

Donovan went to the bridge early in the morning of November 7, wearing ordinary street clothes and shoes. He went to the middle of the span, climbed over the railing and jumped. He landed feet first, went under for a few seconds and then came up out of the water to his waist. He was rescued and taken to the shore. The cold water had chilled him to the bone, so he was immediately given a strong intoxicating beverage. A local newspaper described his condition as follows:

"The effect of a wet outside was counteracted with a wet inside by the aid of the liquid."

A doctor later discovered the daredevil had a broken rib and some minor bruises. Donovan was a lucky man.

By the way, the reporter's reply to Donovan's mother's question was,

"Yes. The Statue of Liberty or the Washington Monument."

"WATER WALKING
Alphonse King with his 'Gold Fish'
Walking on the Niagara River
Below the Falls."

— **Article in the Niagara Falls Gazette,**
Wednesday, December 15, 1886

Alphonse King, 31, a quiet man of small stature, arrived in Niagara Falls, New York, on December 10, 1886 determined to walk on the water below the falls. Yes, walk on the water.

Back in New York City, he had made a substantial wager that he could walk 100 feet on the Niagara River. After all, he had already walked on water in California, Mexico and other places. Why not Niagara Falls?

Now, how could King or anyone walk on water? Was he a saint or magician? No. He simply used a pair of "Gold Fish" shoes. Made of tin, each 30-pound shoe was about 32 inches long, 8 inches wide and 9 inches deep. The upper part looked just like a fish with the head and tailed turned up. An automatic paddle was attached to the flat-bottomed lower part. The shoe was airtight, but had an opening in the center for a foot.

On Saturday morning, December 11, King went into the gorge to win the wager and even cross the entire river. He was told not to perform the stunt from the American side, so he hailed a boat from Canada, got on and went to the other side.

Wearing ordinary street clothes and a silk hat, King examined the scene before putting on the "shoes." A strong chilly mist was blowing from the falls. The sky was overcast. The conditions did not deter him.

At 11 A.M., he began his walk into the history books. A moderate crowd of mostly local people watched from the nearby Upper Suspension Bridge and the gorge banks. They were used to seeing barrels and boats in the river, not water-walkers.

After paddle-walking about 50 feet toward the American side, King met up with a strong current, so he walked downstream for awhile before venturing across again. When he was about one third of the way, a small eddy caught him and forced the shoes together. Down he went, on his face. After his rescue from the icy water, he tried again. This time he fell on his back.

He was now thoroughly drenched and entering the early stages of hypothermia. Having won his wager, he decided to call it a day. The Niagara river had too many unpredictable eddies and strong currents. His shoes only worked in calm water.

"Come up this way,
you'll go through the rapids."

— A call to Alphonse King from a rescue boat

In August of 1887, "Professor" Alphonse King returned to Niagara Falls, not to walk on water, but to test his new "water bicycle." The unusual machine was made of two water-tight zinc cylinders, 10 feet long and 8 inches in diameter and pointed like torpedoes at the ends. A bicycle wheel about 4 feet in diameter was between the cylinders. In the wheel were 24 equally spaced paddles. An ordinary bicycle seat was above the wheel. On either side of the wheel were treadles for the rider's feet. At the stern was a rudder which was controlled with a small "steering wheel."

On August 14, King went into the gorge with his machine. Wearing a suit and silk hat, he didn't look at all like a daredevil. He got on the cycle and began to cross the river at 4:42 P.M. He had to be warned about heading for the Whirlpool Rapids when the cycle was caught by a strong downstream current. He was able to make the correct change in direction and made it to the other side of the river in about 4.5 minutes. He was cheered by the crowds. Success was his.

In admiration of his accomplishment, King was given a gold badge, and the following inscription was put on his cycle:

"Presented to Professor Alphonse King by his Buffalo friends as a token to their admiration of his aquatic skill, Niagara Falls, August 14, 1887."

"He [Oscar Williams] tempted death
to make a spectacle
for the Carnival throngs . . ."

— The Daily Cataract-Journal,
June 15, 1910

Oscar Williams, alias "The Great Houdin" (not be to confused with the magician, Harry Houdini), a 28-year-old painter and steeplejack from Buffalo, New York, had a lot of luck falling. He always survived with minimal injuries. He decided to do something never done at Niagara Falls. He would cross the gorge on a wire, that is, below a wire. He planned to hold on to a strap with his teeth, as a pulley rolled on the wire.

The wire was stretched out near the Upper Steel Arch or Falls View Bridge. It had some slack, but Oscar thought the momentum gained when he went down one end would carry him up the other. The distance across the gorge was about 1,500 feet.

And so, at 5:30 P.M., on June 14, 1910, "The Great Houdin" began his stunt before a crowd estimated to have been 100,000 strong.

Never before had such a mass of humanity been packed together by the gorge.

Williams had trouble going down the wire, at first, but a few swings on his part increased his slide. He passed the area of slack in the middle of the wire, went up a little towards the Canadian side, and then fell back to the middle and stopped.

People rushed closer to the gorge to get a better view of the man stuck over the gorge. Children were separated from their parents. Women fainted.

Meanwhile, Oscar climbed into a rope saddle he took along with him, just for such an emergency. He remained cool in the face of disaster. After spending about 45 minutes dangling over the abyss, a rope was sent out to him, using another pulley.

Hand over hand, he climbed down the rope to the deck of a Maid of the Mist boat. His luck prevailed.

On July 4, 1913, his luck ran out. As he was descending a wire stretched out between two buildings in Mayville, New York, his head crashed into a pole that someone somehow missed seeing when setting up the wire. Oscar's head was crushed, and he died instantly.

"Let her go."

— **Bobby Leach**

Robert "Bobby" Leach, a hotelkeeper from Chippewa, Ontario, who would later be the first man to go over the Horseshoe Fall in a barrel, decided to do something no other daredevil had done — jump from the Upper Steel Arch Bridge with a parachute. To accomplish the stunt, he placed a platform on the middle of the bridge. Above the platform he placed a 30-foot pole, to which the parachute was to be attached.

Despite a strong wind coming from the direction of the falls, Leach was ready to jump in the afternoon of July 1, 1908. A crowd of a few thousand lined the top of the gorge and railing of the bridge. Leach got onto the platform and readied the parachute. The crowd grew quiet.

At 1:05, Bobby dropped like an arrow for about 30 feet, and then the parachute came down and spread open, slowing his descent. It took about 30 seconds to go from the bridge to the water. Bobby splashed into the water and swam towards the Canadian side. Near the shore, he was picked up by the crew of a rescue boat. The applause from the spectators was nearly deafening. Needless to say, Bobby was tickled pink, and he announced his desire to repeat the performance on July 4.

July 4 came and Bobby changed his mind. The applause of spectators was not enough for him. He wanted money, preferably lots of it. He only made about $150 from the first jump.

Since no one would come up with the money, Bobby wouldn't come down from the bridge.

"The spray cut my face so hard
that I had to close my eyes
as it made the dip
and they were shut
when I passed under the bridge."

— Lincoln J. Beachy

Lincoln Beachy started flying dirigibles when he was 18 years-old. But the balloons were not as fast as the new fly machines with wings, so he switched. He soon became an excellent pilot.

On June 27 and 28, 1911, the cities of Niagara Falls, New York, and Niagara Falls, Ontario, held an International Carnival, featuring fireworks, parades and other forms of entertainment. Those running

Lincoln J. Beachy seated in his Curtiss biplane

the affair advertised for some kind of air show. Beachy responded and got the job, for which he would be given a "prize" of $1,000.

He arrived a few days before the Carnival and flew in an air meet at Fort Erie, Ontario, a small community across the river from Buffalo, New York. Then he flew to an air field in Niagara Falls, New York. He was greeted by a crowd of about 5,000.

Beachy piloted a Curtiss biplane called a "pusher." It consisted of a wooden frame, two wings and a 50 horsepower rear engine. Its pilot sat out in the open air.

At 5:40 P.M., on September 27, in a steady light rain, Beachy took off from the field cornered by 9th and Niagara Streets and headed for the falls. Once there, he circled the area a few times and then flew to the head of the Canadian Rapids. From there he descended until he passed about 20 feet over the brink of the Horseshoe Fall and into the cloud of mist.

He emerged from the cloud and dove into the gorge. Just before the Upper Steel Arch Bridge, he hit an air pocket and the plane dropped like an egg. The engine misfired. Beachy fought to regain control. That he did as he passed under the bridge.

In an interview with a reporter after the flight, he sai

"It is a flight that is filled with more dangers than you can imagine. The spray cut my face so hard that I had to close my eyes as I made the dip and they were shut when I passed under the bridge. I was never in such treacherous air currents. You cannot imagine what it means to have the machine totter as mine did unless you have been in one. Right under the bridge the machine came into a vacuum and dropped so fast that it stopped the flow of the gasoline into the carburetor and the engine skipped."

Beachy climbed out of the gorge just before the two railroad bridges. He was well received when he landed at the airfield. He flew again the next day over the falls, but he did not want to go under the bridge again.

On March 14, 1915, after a very successful career as a stunt pilot, Beachy was killed when his German Taube monoplane broke apart in an exhibition flight over San Francisco Bay.

"Go in, I don't need any assistance."

— James Shay to his rescuers from an isle in the American Rapids

James L. Shay, 49, was a decorated veteran of the Spanish War who was known for taking chances. The Niagara Falls, New York, resident was also an athlete. He often went to the state park by the falls to exercise. One day, after rescuing a man from them, he was convinced he could swim across the American Rapids.

And so, Shay made it known that he was going to do the stunt on Labor Day, Monday, September 5, 1927. Wearing a full swim suit with medals on his chest and back, along with sneakers with sharpened spikes on the soles, he eluded the park police all afternoon. They were determined to stop him.

He wanted to start off from the mainland, but it was being watched too carefully, so he went to Green Island, the largest island between Goat Island and the mainland. There he entered the water and soon attracted a large crowd _and_ the police.

After being swept off his feet by the currents and slippery river-bed, Shay panicked and ended up taking refuge on a tiny rocky island. He didn't call for help, however. He intended to go on, after a rest.

Meanwhile, a group of firemen and policemen, using safety lines, went after the daredevil. When they neared the islet, Shay tried to avoid them, but they outnumbered him and soon forced him back to Green Island.

Shay was arrested and demanded a jury trial, which he got. He was found guilty and fined about $50. He admitted that it was probably not possible to cross the rapids on foot.

"'Stunting' Woman Plunges to Death Off Bridge Here; Body Is Recovered"

— Niagara Falls Gazette, Saturday, July 7, 1951

A number of people, most of them local residents, have challenged the bridges over the Niagara River gorge. Many of them have died, their bodies either crashing into the jagged rocks of the cliffs or into the lower river.

At about 2:45 A.M., on Saturday, July 7, 1951, Violet May Savery, a cook at an inn in Niagara Falls, Ontario, and Adolph Fuchs, her common law husband, started back home after enjoying a few drinks of "hard liquor" on the American side of the gorge.

Like many local people, they would walk across the Whirlpool Rapids Bridge. When they reached the middle of the span, Violet told Adolph that she could outdo him in acrobatics. Then she climbed the railing and began to walk toward Canada.

After going about 25 feet, Violet suddenly fell. Adolph lunged toward her and was able to grab her arms. He held on and shouted for help. Help came from the Canadian side. A bridge toll collector, customs officer and immigration officer ran as fast as possible. Just when they arrived on the scene, Adolph lost his grip and Violet fell.

Violet's body was found later that morning floating face down at the mouth of the river, near Youngstown. It was recovered by the U.S. Coast Guard.

"I wouldn't suggest that any novices try it."

— Brent Scott, balloonist

On Friday, July 13, "Friday the 13th," 1984, two "ifo's" (identified flying objects) hovered over Niagara Falls. Tourists and local residents were amazed by the sight.

What were the "ifo's?" Hot-air balloons. The balloonists, Brent Scott, 31, from San Angelo, Texas, and Joseph Heartsill, 33, from Meridian, Texas, claimed they had permission from the FAA or U.S. Federal Aviation Agency. That doesn't sound true, because sightseeing helicopters frequent the skies over the falls, following definite flight paths. Balloons would obviously get in the way.

The two balloons descended right over the cataracts, nearly touching them. *That* was both dangerous and foolish. Then they went into the gorge from the Rainbow Bridge to the Whirlpool Rapids Bridge. It was there that Scott said,

"We actually touched the river."

That wasn't all that was touched.

"I feel OK, except for my throat.
I'm having a little trouble swallowing."

— John Wooten

John Wooten, self-proclaimed "World's Strongest Man," did some
thing no one ever did at Niagara Falls. He used his head. Actually, he pulled a bus with it.

On Thursday, June 29, 1989, just after 1 P.M., Wooten, 41, pulled
a 13-ton bus over the international boundary line on the Rainbow
Bridge. He used a rope, one end attached to the front bumper; the
other wrapped in a hangman's noose around his neck.

He had hoped to pull the bus 3 or 4 bus lengths, but the surface
was too slippery. He was satisfied with the outcome.

How did he get to be so strong? He said,

> "I do a lot of power lifting. I do not do drugs, and I am
> completely free of any type of steroid. The only thing I
> take are vitamins."

The stunt was over in just five minutes. The spectators were not
all impressed. Wooten gained neither fame or fortune, like nearly all
of Niagara's challengers.

About the Author

Paul Gromosiak, one of the region's most respected Niagara Falls historians, takes great pride in being a life-long Western New Yorker. Born in 1942 in Niagara Falls, New York, Paul's fascination with the Mighty Niagara was sparked at home. His father would often tell him stories about early life on the Niagara Frontier. Paul has been researching Niagara's natural and human past ever since, authoring five books that focus on different aspects of the falls.

When people want to know about the Falls, they look to Gromosiak. He is frequently interviewed by both local and national media, appearing on CBS and in a PBS documentary called *Fading in the Mist.* Canada's weekly newsmagazine MacLean's even interviewed him about the custom of honeymooning at the Falls.

Gromosiak's articles have appeared in the *Buffalo News,* the *Niagara Gazette* and other publications. His books include: *Niagara Falls Q & A, Answers to the 100 Most Common Questions about Niagara Falls, Soaring Gulls and Bowing Trees: The History of the Islands Above the Falls, Zany Niagara: The Funny Things People Say About Niagara Falls and Water Over the Falls: 101 of the Most Memorable Events at Niagara Falls.*

The author graduated from Niagara University in 1964 with a B.S. in Chemistry. He has worked as a chemistry teacher in the Niagara Falls School District and as a chemist for Eastman Kodak Company and Hooker Chemical Corporation. Among his interests: hiking and listening to a variety of music.

Birth of a Publishing Company

T he Buffalo area's most innovative publishing celebrated its 19th anniversary in 2003 by hitting a benchmark that few regional publishing houses achieve. Western New York Wares Inc. has moved more than 165,000 books and other regional products into homes, schools and libraries around the world.

If all these books were laid cover-to-cover starting at the foot of Main Street near HSBC Center, the trail would stretch past the UB South Campus, snake through Williamsville, Clarence and end somewhere beyond Akron Falls Park! Putting it a different way, we've printed and distributed about 19 million pages of information about our region.

A pretty impressive path for a company that sprouted its roots in trivial turf!

The year was 1984 and the trivia craze was taking the nation by storm. As Buffalo journalist Brian Meyer played a popular trivia game with friends in his North Buffalo living room, he envisioned a game that tests players' knowledge about people and events in their hometown. Western New York Trivia Quotient sold out its first edition in six weeks and established Meyer as an up-and-coming young entrepreneur.

A year later, he compiled a book of quotations that chronicled the feisty reign of Mayor Jimmy Griffin. Meyer refuses to disclose how many six-packs were consumed while sifting through hundreds of "Griffinisms." An updated volume was published during Griffin's last year in office.

Meyer, a City Hall reporter for the Buffalo News, spent 15 years at WBEN Radio where he served a managing editor. As founder and president of Western New York Wares Inc., Meyer has collaborated with dozens of authors, artists and photographers. By 2003, the region's premier publisher of local books had been involved in publishing, marketing or distributing more than 100 regional products.

The Buffalo native is a graduate of the Marquette University, St. Joseph's Collegiate Institute and Buffalo Public School #56. He teaches communications courses at Buffalo State College and Medaille College. Meyer is treasurer of the Greater Buffalo Society of Professional Journalists' Scholarship Fund.

Meyer is assisted by Michele Ratzel, the company's business manager, and Tom Connolly, manager of marketing and distribution. The trio has more than 40 years of cumulative experience in the regional publishing arena.

Connolly works as a news anchor and producer at WBEN Radio. He co-authored *Hometown Heroes: Western New Yorkers in Desert Storm*. Ratzel works at the Park School of Buffalo.

Internet Site Focuses on Local History, Sports, Weather and Tourist Attractions

www. wnybooks.com

Our unique web site is a treasure trove of information for those who enjoy learning about the people, places and events that have shaped Western New York.

The site showcases full-color photography some of the region's most respected shutterbugs and literary passages from many best-selling regional books. The works of more than 30 local authors, photographers and game inventors are included.

Browsers will enjoy meandering through the many "departments" of our cyberspace bookstore:

Niagara Falls: The history and magnetism of this natural wonder spring to life on our web site. Learn more about daredevils who defied the Mighty Niagara, humorous happenings and unusual historical facts.

Nature: Enjoy a stunning visual celebration of Western New York's natural treasures. Full color photographs and vividly written descriptions will spur many adventurers to explore these wonders firsthand.

Ghosts/Supernatural: East Aurora author Mason Winfield shares some "ghostly" insights into paranormal happenings in Western New York.

Weather: Channel 7 weather guru Tom Jolls chronicles many of the most memorable, humorous and dramatic tales about Buffalo's four seasons.

Sports: Buffalo Bills photographs spring to life, courtesy of respected photographer Robert L. Smith. Savor some of the greatest moments in football history as the chief photographer for the Bills takes fans on a visual roller coaster road that spans three decades.

The Internet site also showcases regional books for children, architectural guides and walking tours.

www.wnybooks.com

Other Regional Books

Visit our Web site at www.Buffalobooks.com for a complete list of titles distributed by Western New York Wares Inc.

Goat Island – A unique look at the historic and picturesque islands of Niagara Falls. Paul Gromosiak includes riveting true-to-life tales about the Hermit of Goat Island, the Cave of the Winds and daredevil feats. Includes a map for walking tours and color photos.
ISBN: 1-879201-43-7   *$9.95*

Nature's Niagara: A Walk on the Wild Side — Learn more about the wild animals, plants and geological formations at Niagara Falls. Written by Paul Gromosiak, the book includes many full-color photographs and maps.
ISBN: 1-879201-31-3   *$8.95*

Niagara Falls Q&A: Answers to the 100 Most Common Questions About Niagara Falls — Author Paul Gromosiak spent four summers chatting with 40,000 Falls tourists. This invaluable guide answers 100 commonly-asked questions. The book also includes photos, many of them in color.
ISBN: 0-9620314-8-8   *$4.50*

Water Over the Falls: 101 of the Most Memorable Events at Niagara Falls — Daredevils who defied the Mighty Niagara. Tragic rock slides and heroic rescues. More than 100 true-to-life tales are chronicled by local historian Paul Gromosiak. Color photos and vintage black-and-white photos.
ISBN: 1-879201-16-X   *$8.99*

Zany Niagara: The Funny Things People Say About Niagara Falls — A lighthearted tour of humorous happenings and historical oddities. Penned by Paul Gromosiak and illustrated by John Hardiman.
ISBN: 1-879201-06-2   *$4.95*

Exploring Niagara: The Complete Guide to Niagara Falls and Vicinity — Filled with 77 spectacular full-color photos, the guide includes dozens of wineries, canals, waterfalls and mansions. Authors Hans and Allyson Tammemagi also chronicle the history that shaped the region.
ISBN: 0-9681815-0-3   *$14.25*

Niagara Falls — One of the world's most spectacular natural wonders springs to life in a book that contains more than 150 color photographs. From a visit in 1678 when a missionary recorded the first eyewitness account of the Falls, to an autumn day in 1993 when Dave Mundy became the only person to survive two barrel rides over the Mighty Niagara, readers experience an exhilarating armchair tour. The book also includes chapters on the Niagara Gorge, Niagara-on-the-Lake, wineries, the famous floral clock and Fort Erie.
ISBN: 2-84339-023-0   *$9.99*

The Magic of Niagara — Viewing the Mighty Niagara for the first time stirs images of tranquility, power and magic. The story of Niagara is 12,000 years old, and author George Bailey skillfully captures the historical highlights in a book that contains a riveting text and more than 100 photographs. Sections include Niagara in the winter, the Maid of the Mist, famous daredevils and the Niagara Parks Butterfly Conservancy.
ISBN: 0-9682635-0-X   *$15.99*

This is Niagara Falls — Vibrant color photographs — more than 50 of them — capture the power and majesty of the Mighty Niagara. From the moment when darkness descends on this wonder and a dazzling display of lights appears, to the instant when the Maid of the Boat inches close to the foamy base of the Falls, this book captures the mystique of a this natural wonder.
ISBN: 1-879201-38-0   *$7.98*

Toronto and Niagara Falls — Two world-renowned destinations are showcased in one photo-packed book! More than 240 full-color photographs, a detailed street map, informative text and user-friendly index make this an invaluable companion. Readers will explore Chinatown, museums, mansions, forts and gardens in Toronto. The Niagara Falls section highlights such attractions as Cave of the Winds, Maid of the Mist and Skylon Tower.
ISBN: 88-8029-569-1   *$15.99*

Victorian Buffalo: Images From the Buffalo and Erie County Public Library — Visit Buffalo as it looked in the 19th century through steel engravings, woodcuts, lithography and other forms of nonphotographic art. Author Cynthia VanNess has selected scenes that showcase everyday life and views of historic structures created by luminaries like Frank Lloyd Wright, Louis Sullivan and E.B. Green.
ISBN: 1-879201-30-5 *$13.95*

The Erie Canal: The Ditch That Opened a Nation — Despite its shallow depths, the waters of the Erie carry an amazing history legacy. It was in canal towns like Lockport and Tonawanda where the doors to the American frontier were unlocked. Written by Daniel T. Murphy, the book includes dozens of photos.
ISBN: 1-879201-34-8 *$8.95*

Erie Canal Legacy: Architectural Treasures of the Empire State — Photographer Andy Olenick and author Richard O. Reisem take readers on a 363-mile journey along the canal route. This hardcover book is comprised of full-color photos and an enlightening text.
ISBN: 0-9641706-6-3 *$39.95*

National Landmarks of Western New York: Famous People and Historic Places — Gracious mansions and thundering waterfalls. Battleships and nostalgic fireboats. Power plants and Indian long houses. Author Jan Sheridan researched nearly 30 National Historic Landmarks in the Buffalo-Niagara and Finger Lakes regions. Dozens of photographs, maps and a comprehensive index.
ISBN: 1-879201-36-4 *$9.95*

Beyond Buffalo: A Photographic Journey and Guide to the Secret Natural Wonders of our Region — Full color photographs and informative vignettes showcase 30 remarkable sites. Author David Reade also includes directions and tips for enjoying each site.
ISBN: 1-879201-19-4 *$19.95*

Western New York Weather Guide — Readers won't want any "winteruptions" as they breeze through this lively book written by former Channel 7 weather guru Tom Jolls. Co-authored by Brian Meyer and Joseph VanMeer, the book focuses on historic and humorous weather events over the past century.
ISBN: 1-879201-18-1 *$7.95*

White Death: Blizzard of '77 — This 356-page softcover book chronicles one of the region's most dramatic historical events. Written by Erno Rossi, the book includes more than 60 photographs.
ISBN: 0-920926-03-7 *$16.95*

Great Lake Effects: Buffalo Beyond Winter and Wings — a unique cookbook that is filled with intriguing historical facts about the region. The hardcover book has been compiled by the Junior League of Buffalo.
ISBN: 1-879201-18-1 *$18.95*

Buffalo Treasures: A Downtown Walking Guide — Readers are led on a fascinating tour of 25 major buildings. A user-friendly map and dozens of illustrations by Kenneth Sheridan supplement an enlightening text by Jan Sheridan.
ISBN: 1-879201-15-1 *$4.95*

Church Tales of the Niagara Frontier: Legends, History & Architecture — This first-of-a-kind book traces the rich history and folklore of the region through accounts of 60 area churches and places of worship. Written by the late Austin M. Fox and illustrated by Lawrence McIntyre.
ISBN : 1-879201-13-5 *$14.95*

Symbol & Show: The Pan-American Exposition of 1901 — A riveting look at perhaps the greatest event in Buffalo's history. Written by the late Austin M. Fox and illustrated by Lawrence McIntyre, this book offers a lively assessment of the Exposition, bringing to light many half-forgotten facts.
ISBN: 1-879201-33-X *$15.95*

Frank Lloyd Wright's Darwin D. Martin House: Rescue of a Landmark— The untold story of the abandonment and rescue of the region's most architecturally-significant home is recounted in vivid detail by Marjorie L. Quinlan. The book includes color photos and detailed architectural plans.
ISBN: 1-879201-32-1 *$13.95*

Buffalo's Brush With the Arts: From Huck Finn to Murphy Brown — A fascinating adventure behind the manuscripts and million-dollar book deals, highlighting the Niagara Frontier's connection to many creative geniuses. Authored by Joe Marren, the book contains more than 20 photographs from the Courier-Express Collection.
ISBN: 1-879201-24-0   *$7.95*

Classic Buffalo: A Heritage of Distinguished Architecture — A stunning hardcover book pays tribute to the region's architectural heritage. Striking full-color photographs by Andy Olenick and an engaging text by Richard O. Reisem make this coffee-table book a keepsake for history buffs.
ISBN: 0-9671480-06   *$39.95*

Spirits of the Great Hill: More Haunted Sites and Ancient Mysteries of Upstate New York — From Mark Twain's Buffalo ghost, to Houdini's Halloween, Mason Winfield pens a riveting sequel to his supernatural survey of the region.
ISBN: 1-879201-35-6   *$13.95*

Shadows of the Western Door: Haunted Sites and Ancient Mysteries of Upstate New York — A supernatural safari across Western New York. Guided by the insights of modern research, author Mason Winfield pens a colorful, provocative and electrifying study of the paranormal.
ISBN: 1-829201-22-4   *$13.95*

A Ghosthunter's Journal: Tales of the Supernatural and the Strange in Upstate New York — A delightfully diverse smorgasbord of strange encounters, all of them set in Western New York. The 13 fictional stories are inspired by the files of Mason Winfield.
ISBN: 1-879201-29-1   *$12.95*

John D. Larkin: A Business Pioneer — The riveting story of a Buffalo man who built a small soap manufacturing outfit into one of the largest mail order houses in the nation. Daniel I. Larkin, a grandson of John D. Larkin, has penned a book that reflects on the American dream at its best.
ISBN: 0-9619697-1-7   *$14.95*

Buffalo's Waterfront : A Guidebook — Edited by Tim Tielman, this user-friendly guide showcases more than 100 shoreline sites. It includes a handy fold-out map. Published by the Preservation Coalition of Erie County.
ISBN: 1-879201-00-3   *$5.95*

Bodyslams in Buffalo: The Complete History of Pro Wrestling In Western New York — Author Dan Murphy traces the region's rich wrestling history, from Ilio DiPaolo and Dick "The Destroyer" Beyer, to Adorable Adrian Adonis. Dozens of photos.
ISBN: 1-879201-42-9   *$9.95*

Tale of the Tape: A History of the Buffalo Bills From the Inside — Eddie "Abe" Abramoski reflects on scores on humorous, emotional and enlightening anecdotes that stretch back to the first Bills training camp in East Aurora. Many photos accompany the lively text.
ISBN: 1-879201-41-0   *$10.95*

The Rainbow City: Celebrating Light, Color and Architecture at the Pan-American Exposition, Buffalo 1901 — The story of Buffalo's glorious moment, recounted in 160 pages and more than 20 images. Written by Kerry S. Grant of the University at Buffalo, the book offers a revealing glimpse of an era when Buffalo was the nation's eighth largest city.
ISBN: 0-9671480-5-7   *$39.95*

Please include 8% sales tax for all orders in New York and the following amount for shipping: Under $25: $3.00
$25-$49: $4.00
$50 or more: $5.00

Visit our Web site at: www.Buffalobooks.com or write for a catalog:

Western New York Wares Inc.
P.O. Box 733
Ellicott Station
Buffalo, New York 14205